CREATING HIGH PERFORMANCE CLASSROOM GROUPS

CREATING HIGH PERFORMANCE CLASSROOM GROUPS

NINA W. BROWN, Ed.D.
PROFESSOR OF COUNSELING
OLD DOMINION UNIVERSITY
NORFOLK, VIRGINIA

FALMER PRESS
A MEMBER OF THE TAYLOR & FRANCIS GROUP
NEW YORK & LONDON
2000

Published in 2000 by
Falmer Press
A Member of the Taylor & Francis Group
29 West 35th Street
New York, NY 10001

10   9   8   7   6   5   4   3   2   1

Library of Congress Cataloging-in-Publication Data is available from the
Library of Congress.

Creating high performance classroom groups / by
    Nina W. Brown

        Includes index.
        ISBN 0-8153-3689-6
        ISBN 0-8153-3690-X (paperback)

Printed on acid-free, 250-year-life paper.
Manufactured in the United States of America

*This book is dedicated to Nicholas Francis and Emma Brown,
the two newest members of the family.*

Contents

CREATING HIGH PERFORMANCE CLASSROOM GROUPS

CHAPTER 1

Why Classroom Groups?

INTRODUCTION

Two colleagues, professors in engineering and geology, respectively, independently approached me to ask about forming and conducting classroom groups. As we discussed the topic, it became clear to me that this was a complex undertaking for instructors with no background in group work, and that they had few resources available for guidance. A review of the available resources and books revealed that they:

- Seemed to lack enough specificity to guide instructors who have teaching content as their primary concern
- Did not provide enough rationale for suggested practices
- Did not provide guidelines to direct a student leader through the developmental stages of a group
- Did not give enough direction for structuring the experience to prevent some common problems
- Did not provide strategies to address problems

This book grew out of those discussions with my colleagues and an attempt to give them enough structure and encouragement to use groups effectively in their courses. My experiences with classroom groups and teaching group counseling also contributed to the genesis of this book. Experiences with psychoeducational groups, training groups, and counseling and therapy groups gave me a wide variety of group experiences to draw from in formulating the concepts, ideas, and strategies presented in this book.

GROUPS FOR COOPERATIVE LEARNING

A review of the literature revealed considerable interest in cooperative learning methods, as evidenced by the large number of articles and books on this topic. Cooperative learning takes many forms, and group work is only one method. However, there is a need to teach students how to work effectively in groups in addition to learning content. Increased emphasis on teamwork in many work settings is fueling the search for employees who have these skills and abilities. Yet many, if not most, classrooms emphasize independent student work. Few teach students how to be effective group members or how to be group leaders while still concentrating on task accomplishment. Further, many students report that they "hate" working in groups and/or that they have had no experience working in a group. Some report that they prefer to work independently because it is too frustrating and time consuming to try to work with others. Thus, from day one, instructors who want to use classroom groups face considerable student resistance in addition to their own lack of knowledge about groups.

This book is intended for college instructors who have their subject matter as the primary focus for the class and who want to use classroom groups to enhance the learning process and to teach students how to be effective team or group members and leaders. It is recommended that an instructor read the entire book before trying to use groups for a class; then the various chapters can be reviewed as resources. It may also be helpful for instructors to give student group leaders a copy of the book so that they can have a resource that goes into some detail about situations, conditions, and expectations for the group and leader. In this way the group leader gets instruction and support from two sources, the instructor and a book. The emphasis of this book is on teaching and learning, with considerable attention to structuring group work that can be done independently, that is, not just in the particular classroom during class time. Out-of-class meetings are necessary in many instances if a project is to be accomplished and if the instructor is not always present.

An increasingly common situation occurs when teams or groups are linked electronically. Structuring and directing these groups call for different assumptions and strategies than those used for groups whose members meet face to face.

Problem behaviors on the part of members can be expected. How these are manifested, when they will emerge, and what to do about them are important pieces of information. Information that is not generally presented includes the expected behaviors and attitudes of members associated with stagse of group development. This book presents this information so that both student leaders and instructors can have a selection of responses that take into account personalities, communication, and emotions for both the leader and members, as well as the stage of the group's development.

Another topic in this book that is not usually addressed is that of group-level problems. These can be confusing and frustrating for the leader, and can erode his or her self-confidence. This book presents ways to recognize when there is a group-level problem, as well as suggestions for identifying times when the best strategy is for the leader to understand what is occurring and to manage his or her personal anxiety rather than jumping in too quickly, and when the problem needs to be addressed directly and immediately.

The remainder of this chapter presents definitions of different types of learning groups, ethical considerations for experiential learning, and criteria for distinguishing between effective and ineffective classroom groups. The chapter concludes with topical outlines for subsequent chapters.

DIFFERENT TYPES OF LEARNING GROUPS

Work Groups

Work groups are characterized by:

- Interdependence
- Individual work
- Shared information
- A strong, clearly focused leader who is appointed
- Tasks that emphasize individual contributions and responsibility

This description applies to many classroom groups, whose final product is the result of individual efforts. Members meet to share information, individuals assume responsibility only for their part of the work or product, and members do not work together to problem-solve as part of the task per se, although they may do so for shared resources—for example, computer access. Further, accountability focuses on individuals, whether each member receives a separate grade for his or her contribution, or each member receives a grade based on the quality of the product.

Teams

Teams are characterized by the following:

- Shared leadership
- Interdependence
- Specific roles and functions for members
- Awareness of who is a member and who is not
- A limited life span
- Accountability for individuals and for the group
- Meetings that are open-ended and devoted to problem solving

Classroom groups also share some of these characteristics; that is, members have specific roles and functions, awareness of who is a member and who is not, and a limited life span.

Learning Groups

Learning groups, such as those used in a classroom, tend to be a combination of work groups and teams. Members are peers working together to acquire knowledge and skills and each member contributes, or is expected to contribute, to the product or outcome. Johnson and Johnson (1994) classify learning groups as one of three types:

- Problem-solving
- Special purpose
- Self-management

Problem-solving Groups

Problem-solving groups work on tasks to improve quality, efficiency, and work environment. These groups form to develop strategies or propose solutions to previously identified problems. Examples of problem-solving groups in the classroom are those that are given hypothetical problems, so that the group's task is to develop solutions like those used in Guided Design, and those that are working on research projects.

Other Groups

Special-purpose groups design and introduce reforms, new technology, new processes, and the like. This category includes groups like task forces that are convened to work on a specific issue for a limited time, with an expected outcome of guidance through change or introduction of something new.

Self-management groups have the goal of producing an entire product or service. In the classroom, this type of group oversees a project from beginning to end—for example, deciding on the topic of focus and developing the product, such as a report.

Katzenbach and Smith (1993) fuse two of the types described earlier; they consider teams to be work groups. They classify teams according to function—for example, recommending, making or doing things, or running or directing something. Teams that recommend include groups like:

- Task forces
- Project groups
- Audit or safety groups

Teams that make or do things include groups like:

- Quality circles
- Manufacturing groups
- Sports groups

Teams that run things can be:

- Departments
- Divisions
- Executive committees
- Boards

Classroom groups probably fall under recommending teams, since project groups are included in this category.

CHARACTERISTICS OF EFFECTIVE CLASSROOM GROUPS

Ideal learning or classroom groups are described by Johnson and Johnson (1992, 1997) as having the following characteristics:

- A clearly defined goal
- Cooperative or collaborative structure
- Shared responsibilities
- Communication among members, and between members and an instructor
- Use of consensus for decision making
- Use of members' expertise and skills
- Openness to controversy and conflict
- Cohesiveness
- A sense of trust among members
- Acceptance and support of members
- Expectations of individual responsibility and accountability
- Members with strong interpersonal skills

Each of the above characteristics is briefly described in the following section.

Clearly Defined Goal

A clearly defined goal is essential if a learning group is to be effective. What are members supposed to accomplish? What is the purpose of this group? Is there an expected product? How is the product to be presented? These and other questions must be answered if the group's goal is to be clearly defined and understood. An instructor has to do considerable planning and preparation prior to using groups in classes.

Multiple goals can be confusing. Although an instructor may wish to have both affective and cognitive goals, it may be better to have only one primary goal for class groups. For example, the affective goal for a group project could be increasing students' interest in and expertise at working collaboratively, and the cognitive goal could be increased knowledge of a particular subject. Achieving both of these goals is ideal, but since the strategies used to accomplish them may be very different, having two primary goals may lead to considerable confusion. Giving one goal priority allows selection of specific strategies, evaluation processes, and measurements of success. The other goal is secondary: commendable if it occurs, but not crucial to success for the group. For many courses, the affective goal of learning to work in groups would be secondary.

Cooperative or Collaborative Structure

Some writers refer to cooperative structure, others to collaborative. Both terms highlight the need for interdependence on the part of group members. Interdependence has both an individual and a group component. The individual has a sense of belonging to the group and personal connection to other group members. The group component refers to individuals working together effectively as a smoothly functioning unit, well integrated on several levels. Members who feel included in the group are more inclined to work to accomplish group goals, and the structure of the group can contribute to their sense of belonging and hence willingness to participate. Cooperative and/or collaborative structure for classroom groups requires an instructor to develop, monitor, and revise as needed guidelines for how members are to behave, interact, and work together. Guidelines can specify such details as when group meetings will be held and under what circumstances (e.g., prohibiting impromptu meetings where all members cannot be present); how, by whom, and when work will be done; or how to submit periodic reports of progress.

Communication

Communication among members is certainly a part of any cooperative structure. Members judge their degree of inclusion or exclusion in part by the quality and quantity of their communication with the group. Encouraging members to work out conflicts and deal with controversy constructively leads to greater satisfaction with the group and an improved product.

Selecting a leader who leads by example, who understands that the group members are peers working cooperatively to accomplish a task, and who seeks input from all members also facilitates group process. A group leader who gives orders and expects obedience will not get the degree of cooperation and open lines of communication that a leader who seeks to work cooperatively will.

Another line of communication runs between the instructor and the group. The instructor is the guide, facilitator, expert, and evaluator. Group members expect the instructor to:

- Be available for consultation
- Provide clarification
- Answer questions
- Provide information
- Help work out problems

The instructor cannot expect to give the group its task, and then fade from the picture.

Shared Responsibilities

Shared responsibilities contribute to cooperative structure. A group leader has both task and maintenance functions, but does not have sole responsibility for successful functioning of the group; members share some responsibility for the group. Members can:

- Help work out conflicts
- Provide information and/or needed clarification
- Attend and listen to each other
- Summarize when needed
- Help take care of gatekeeping duties such as time limits

While it is best to have a designated leader, that individual can be more effective if he or she allows other members to take some responsibility for the group. Similarly, the group leader does not assume the group's success as his or her own, but acknowledges that success is due to all members' contributions.

Consensual Decision Making

Learning groups function better when decisions are made by consensus rather than by authority, majority vote, or default. Decisions by an authority, such as the group leader, are seen as dictatorial and devaluing the opinions of group members. (There are times when the authority of the instructor has to prevail, but those times should be few.)

Voting, subject to the will of the majority, sets up a win-lose situation. Under these circumstances, the losers are disgruntled and less likely to work to implement the decision. Further, there are times when the majority may not make an informed, thoughtful decision. The majority decision is not always the best or correct one.

Avoiding a decision is, by default, making a decision, but this approach leads to confusion and uncertainty. This decision-making strategy seldom results in progress for the group.

Using consensus to make decisions is more time consuming, but usually results in decisions that group members are committed to. Members feel that their opinions were heard and considered as part of the decision, and thus they feel a part of the process. One important difficulty with using consensus in classroom groups is that members may need to be taught how to participate effectively in consensus building.

Members' Expertise

Participants in classroom groups should understand from the very beginning that each person has something to contribute, and the group is expected to capitalize on the expertise and skill of each member. Because every member will have different areas of expertise and skill, the constructive and creative use of differences will make the group more successful.

If each member is to contribute, this expectation must be a part of the plan the group develops. Further, it is important that regularly scheduled meetings be held so that members can provide input, request needed assistance, alert others to problems, and give and receive support. It is devastating to a group to find out at a late date that something is not done, or that there is a serious problem.

Instructors can facilitate proper use of members' expertise and skill by requiring groups to submit plans that state specifically what each member is to contribute to the final product. It may not hurt to get signatures indicating that each member has read the plan and agrees with it. At this point, the instructor can intervene if the workload is not evenly distributed, or if some members have inconsequential tasks. All members should assume significant parts of the task.

Another strategy is to have the group review the task and list the various skills and expertise that will be needed, such as computer graphics. This allows members to volunteer any specialized knowledge or skill. It has the additional advantage of alerting members to an absent area of expertise or skill, so they can make plans to learn it, or to secure it in some way.

Controversy and Conflict

Controversy and conflict are present in all groups in varying degrees of intensity and overtness. These differences in opinions, perspectives, and values can be used constructively, as long as they are aired and worked through. Open conflicts that are not worked through can be detrimental to how members feel about the group and to the quality of their participation. Hidden conflicts are even more detrimental to the group, as they are not readily available to be resolved, but undermine the cohesiveness of the group in indirect and subtle ways. Trying to suppress or deny conflict does not keep it from affecting the group. Helping members acknowledge and work through conflict not only helps the group function more effectively, but also teaches members that conflicts, properly handled, are not destructive. Such an approach also models methods of conflict resolution.

Cohesiveness

Group cohesion develops over time and characterizes effective and productive groups that achieve both group and individual goals. Members are committed to a cohesive group, to not only its task but also its group members; they assume personal responsibility for the group and its outcome and are more willing to defend the group against attack or criticism.

Cohesive group members feel a sense of solidarity, value the group and its members, allow controversy to emerge, deal with conflict constructively, and provide mutual trust and support. Members show their commitment to the group by low absenteeism and turnover. Morale is high in cohesive groups.

Cohesiveness is desirable in groups because it promotes productivity. It occurs after members understand the task and their roles in accomplishing it, feel safe and valued, and know that controversy and conflict can be tolerated and effectively managed.

Trust

Trust develops in a group when members feel safe, cared for, valued, and accepted. Members need to feel that they will not be attacked, demeaned, or hurt. Instructors can promote safety by supplying structure for groups, guidelines for performance, and instructions for how the group is to function. Careful monitoring also helps foster development of an "emotionally safe" group environment.

Group leaders can also be helpful by:

- Insuring that all members have an opportunity for input
- Setting a norm that members are listened to with respect
- Blocking attacks or demeaning remarks
- Making sure that meetings are held when all members can attend

The session-to-session responsibility for promoting safety and trust in the group belongs to the group leader.

Acceptance and Support

Effective groups are characterized by members who accept and support each other. Groups bond around similarities and dissolve around differences. This principle underscores the importance of members' understanding of their similarities. The more they perceive that they are different, the less they will offer acceptance and support.

Unfortunately, most classroom groups do not take the time and effort needed to help group members search out and understand similarities. Instead, in a classroom group, members usually focus on obvious differences and react accordingly. The instructor can help by pointing out similarities, using exercises to help members get to know each other, and emphasizing the importance of acceptance and mutual support for group members.

Responsibility and Accountability

Many group members fear that they will have to accept major responsibility in the group, but will receive little credit for their work. Others may coast because they assume that what they do as an individual will not be noticed, and that others in the group will make sure the work is done. Neither stance is of benefit to the group.

The instructor needs to make clear from the beginning the extent of individual responsibility and accountability, and the methods for evaluating both group and individual contributions. One suggestion is to have both group and individual grades, so that even if the group product is good and an individual's contribution is not, or vice versa, others neither suffer nor benefit.

Interpersonal Skills

Interpersonal skills that are particularly useful in learning or classroom groups are communication and relationship skills. Communication skills are:

- Active listening and responding
- Concreteness
- Clarification
- Constructive confrontation
- Conflict resolution

Relationship skills are:

- Respectfulness
- Tolerance of differences and diversity
- Acceptance
- Constructive feedback

Interpersonal skills promote development of group cohesiveness. These are the behaviors that make members feel valued and supported, promote feelings of safety, and increase a sense of solidarity, all of which lead to commitment to the group and its task. Leaders and members can increase their interpersonal skills as they learn from each other, either directly or through modeling, how to communicate and relate more effectively. The instructor can also play a role in this development, by teaching and modeling some of these skills.

PROFESSIONAL AND ETHICAL RESPONSIBILITIES

As with any class, those classes that use a group or team structure for learning should be guided by professional and ethical responsibilities for both the instructor and the students. The addition of group to other methods of instruction increases the need for attention to certain policies that ensure safety for students and protection for an instructor.

The following list contains the minimum suggested professional and ethical responsibilities for the instructor. Each is briefly described with a rationale for inclusion.

Informed Consent

Informed consent means that participants are notified in advance about intentions, the nature of the contract, and time boundaries. Participants enter into the activity with these minimum understandings so that they have an opportunity to make personal judgments about their abilities and the suitability of the proposed activity to meet their needs.

The instructor can meet this responsibility with a carefully constructed syllabus, a review of class requirements, detailed guidelines for student participation and evaluation, and provision of some means for receiving feedback from students. Giving students adequate information allows them to make better decisions about their participation.

Required Participation

This is a part of informed consent but is discussed separately because of its relation to group work in a class. Required participation in a group can be a part of a class, but the instructor should take care to spell out the behaviors that he or she will evaluate to determine a student's degree of participation. This is especially important if participation is a part of the grade. (This topic is presented more fully in Chapters 2 and 3.)

Freedom of Choice

Students, by definition, are involuntary participants. On the surface they have the freedom to participate or not participate, but the reality is that they have very little or no choice, since participation is typically a required part of a course and most courses are required as part of their studies for a degree. Therefore, with some degree of participation as a given, it is important for the instructor to allow students to make the decision about the level of their participation and, more importantly, to ensure that students in groups are not subjected to pressure to go beyond their self-imposed limits. Students should not be pushed to self-disclose or made to feel wrong or inadequate if they do not do so. The instructor can address this concern in the written guidelines for group members and by emphasizing this point when reviewing class requirements.

Confidentiality

It is important for the instructor to describe the procedures for maintaining confidentiality. Students offer numerous personal disclosures in almost every class, whether to the entire class or to the instructor alone. The instructor should expect that self-disclosure of personal material will occur in group work. Considerable damage, however, can result from betrayal of confidences, leading to mistrust and feelings of being in danger. Group members need to know from the beginning just what material cannot and will not be kept confidential. The instructor should be considered a de facto member of every class group and this should be stated on the syllabus, in the guidelines for groups, and as part of the review of course requirements. In other words, one instance in which confidentiality does not apply is to the instructor. The instructor should be kept as fully informed as possible. Personal disclosures not relevant to the class need not be reported to the instructor, but any violations of university or class policies, or of public laws, must be. There may also be instances when the instructor will have to break confidentiality because of ethical, legal, or professional reasons. In such situations the instructor should make it clear that a student will be informed in advance of any disclosure to officials.

Instructor-Imposed Values

Respect for differing values is an important concept for instructors to model. Care should be taken that the instructor's values are not imposed. These values can be communicated when appropriate, but there should be no demands that students assume these values. This is especially important because most classes have considerable racial, ethnic, gender, religious, and social class diversity.

Student Responsibilities

Students not only have rights, they also have responsibilities. Here, "responsibilities" are defined in a more general sense than when used to mean expectations for performance and demeanor in class. In this instance, responsibilities are more like the ethical and professional responsibilities of instructors. Following are some suggestions for defining and applying responsibilities in a class that uses group work.

- Violations of policies; honor pledge—Students have the responsibility to report to the instructor violations of the institution's policies on racial and sexual harassment, and those on alcohol and drug use. Students also have the responsibility to act in accordance with the honor pledge for all tests and projects.
- Plagiarism and copyright laws—Students will fully document all sources used in work submitted for a class. Failure to do so is considered plagiarism. Students are also expected to know and abide by copyright laws.
- Authorship of work—Students are expected to submit only work that they developed and completed. Submission of others' work is considered a violation of the honor system. Furthermore, students are expected to obtain a professor's permission in advance of submitting work done for another class. Dual submissions are discouraged but not prohibited if the professor agrees to them.
- Confidentiality—Students are expected to consider personal material revealed in classes, interviews, class exercises, class groups, and so on to be confidential when talking to those outside class. The processes used in classes and their cognitive content can be freely discussed. In the event, however, that university officials, or other similar persons, have legitimate reasons to know personal material, students are expected to disclose as appropriate.
- Respect for the rights of others—Students are expected to respect the rights of other students and not engage in acts that sabotage access to achievement, such as hiding, stealing, or defacing library material; destroying or interfering with laboratory equipment or experiments; deliberately withholding distributed materials; giving false information, and so on. Students must also refrain from any acts of coercion, threats, or harassment.

OVERVIEW OF CHAPTERS

Chapter 2

Chapter 2, "The Challenge of Preparation," describes the fundamentals needed by instructors. Since careful preparation is essential for successful learning, considerable attention is given to the specifics needed for instructors' planning, such as goals and objectives, how the syllabus helps, guidelines for forming groups, and elements for directing and structuring groups. Completing the chapter are exercises that can be used for the first group session, either in the classroom or in individual groups.

Chapter 3

Chapter 3, "Organizing and Guiding," expands and elaborates on how to construct a syllabus to facilitate the use of groups. Guidelines are presented for projects and tasks for groups. Sample course syllabus outlines are included in the chapter.

If any single component can be designated as crucial to the success of classroom groups, it is the instructor. The remainder of Chapter 3 describes the various roles an instructor assumes and how these change over the life span of the class. Specifics are given for:

- Planning
- Holding group leader meetings
- How to use the minutes of group sessions
- Teaching and modeling group leadership skills and
- What to expect in the later stages of group

Chapter 4

Chapter 4, "Developing Student Expertise," explains to students how to be effective group members. Presented are 14 attitudes and behaviors that characterize active participation and effective group members, and 16 attitudes and behaviors that characterize ineffective group members. Both sets of behaviors and attitudes are specific enough so that students can easily understand what is expected of them. The descriptions can also be of help to the instructor when observing groups and giving feedback, for they are stated in terms of observable behaviors.

Chapter 5

Chapter 5, "The Group Performance Curve," describes the fundamental characteristics and skills needed to facilitate groups effectively. The chapter was written with both the student group leader and the inexperienced instructor using groups in mind. Rationales are provided for each characteristic and skill.

The instructor will find helpful the discussion on the various ways to select a group leader, as both pros and cons for each method are presented. Also included are preparing the group leader, how to prepare the project or task to be assumed by the group, group facilitation guidelines, and stages of group development. The last topic, group stages, describes expected member and group behaviors over the life span of the group and makes suggestions for actions needed at each stage.

Chapter 6

Chapter 6, "Conflict: Inevitable and Manageable," begins with a definition and description of conflict and presents a schema for levels of conflict, from mild to severe. The novice group leader may be unsure when to step in and when to let matters take their course; presented are indicators not only for when intervention can be of benefit, but also for deciding at what point (e.g., early or late) in the conflict to intervene. Specific leader skills to help diffuse emotional intensity and promote participants' working through the conflict are also described.

A specific conflict intervention strategy is included, with a script and step-by-step directions. The chapter concludes with a discussion on how to identify disguised or masked conflict.

Chapter 7

Chapter 7, "Problem Behaviors and Interventions," deals with common problem behaviors that are encountered in classroom groups, such as silence, monopolizing, poor performance, harassment, and aggressiveness. Interventions that can be used by the novice leader are presented, as are strategies for the instructor. The chapter also gives guidelines the instructor can use when holding individual conferences with students who have exhibited problem behaviors.

Chapter 8

Chapter 8, "Group-Level Problems and Solutions," helps the leader understand when the problem is not at the individual level but at the group level. Sometimes a leader cannot pinpoint just what any one particular member or set of members is doing that causes the group to be uncomfortable. This is most likely due to something consensual among group members, producing a group-level problem. If the leader were to try and intervene on a member level, nothing would change and things might get worse.

Common group-level problems, including anxiety, boredom, withdrawal, and hostility are described with examples. Intervention strategies are presented that address both the feelings and the behaviors of the group leader and the actions that can be taken for the group.

Chapter 9

Chapter 9, "Relating Characteristics and Communication Skills," is about how to promote effective learning in groups using these particular interpersonal skills. Instructors who do not know how to teach these skills may wish to engage colleagues from other fields, such as counseling, to provide instruction and practice for their students.

The skills presented are both verbal and nonverbal. Verbal communication skills include active listening and responding, clarifying, summarizing, and blocking. The importance of giving constructive feedback is discussed, along with guidelines for how to do so. Nonverbal skills include showing interest, attending, and learning how to read the nonverbal behavior of members.

Chapter 10

Chapter 10, "Group Leadership," focuses on effective group leadership. These skills build on the relating and communication skills presented in Chapter 9, such as blocking, linking, questioning, giving encouragement and support, identifying major themes, being direct, and observing.

Specific applications in group sessions are presented, such as beginning a session, soliciting input, and ending a session.

Chapter 11

Chapter 11, "Group Activities and Exercises," presents an array of activities that novice group leaders can use, with specific instructions for planning and conducting them. The exercises include ice breaker, skills training, and closing activities. Instructions include goals and objectives, maximum numbers of participants, time and materials needed, necessary preparation prior to conducting the exercise, procedures, introducing the exercise, what to observe, and processing questions.

Chapter 12

The final chapter, "Electronically Linked Groups," presents an expanded discussion on such groups, which typically will not meet face to face, and may have members who are physically isolated. In such groups, the instructor has to do considerable planning, structuring, monitoring, directing, and providing for group identity and connections.

Electronically linked groups present challenges for the instructor because of their unique characteristics, including a decreased dependence on unity of time and place, greater anonymity, lack of formal communication, and fewer social constraints. Specific instructions for setting up and conducting such groups are presented.

CHAPTER 2

The Challenge of Preparation

The instructor who intends to incorporate group work into a class has considerable work to do prior to the first session; the first step is to become aware of the scope of the task. If groups are to be effective, the instructor needs to plan for expected and desired outcomes, prevention of problems, and a process for learning. Structure becomes an important consideration. Some structure may already be a part of the particular course and can easily be enhanced to incorporate the use of groups; other courses may need to be completely redesigned for groups to be effective. What follows is a list of the basic considerations for an instructor in planning for classroom groups.

- Goals and objectives
- Syllabus
- Students
- Provisions for evaluating the groups and individuals
- Formation of groups
- Group size
- Physical arrangements
- Directions and guidelines
- Observation and monitoring

These planning considerations are discussed at length, and then the chapter closes with suggestions for what to do during the first group meeting.

GOALS AND OBJECTIVES

Goals are end products—that is, what all the work is supposed to accomplish. It may be helpful for the instructor who is beginning to use groups to develop two sets of goals for the course: the cognitive or content goals, and group goals. For example, the cognitive goal for a course in career education and development might be "to know and be able to effectively use career educational materials and strategies with children, adolescents and adults." The group goal might be "to learn how to effectively function as a member of a learning group and to gain an appreciation for the various talents each member brings to the group."

Other group goals could be:

- Learn to function as team members and understand the importance of team development.
- Learn to balance both people and task needs.
- Learn the value of cooperation and collaboration to enhance productivity.
- Learn how to manage talents, defuse conflicts, and accomplish tasks.
- Learn the process of forming and managing teams.
- Learn effective ways of communicating and relating in groups.

Objectives are derived from goals and have three primary characteristics: specificity, observability, and measurability. Objectives should focus on specifics by delineating and describing the primary learning expected. For example, an objective might be for students to define major terms and concepts used in the course. An instructor should create two to four major goals for each course, and the number of objectives should be limited to the eight or ten most important things to be learned. Thus, the instructor has to decide what is most important for students to learn before class begins.

Objectives should be stated in terms of observable behavior. Terms such as *define, describe, illustrate, apply, evaluate, compute,* and *discuss* (either orally or in writing) are often used when writing objectives rather than terms such as *know, understand,* and *integrate,* as these are internal states that cannot be directly observed but can only be inferred. If an instructor chooses to use a term such as *know,* the objective should also specify how the instructor expects to evaluate accomplishment of the objective. For example, the objective "to understand how group dynamics affect the functioning of a group" is insufficient; "to understand how group dynamics affect the functioning of a group by describing the behavior that reflects each dynamic in weekly journals" addresses both specificity and observability.

Objectives should also be measurable. The most important learning outcomes and the extent to which they were achieved should be assessed in some way. Evaluation needed at the end of class is another reason why it is important to formulate objectives carefully prior to beginning the class. If the instructor has included measurable objectives for group participation, students will know that how they function in the group is important and will be assessed.

THE SYLLABUS

It is important to have a syllabus that provides clear directions and structure for the class, as students may not have access to the instructor at all times to clarify and answer questions. Guidelines for and examples of specific components of an effective syllabus are presented in more detail in Chapter 3. The discussion here focuses on the need and rationale for a carefully constructed syllabus.

The syllabus can be conceived of as a contract between the student and instructor that describes expectations for both. The instructor has the responsibility to structure learning for the class so that students achieve the expected learning outcomes and are aware of what their contributions to learning will be (e.g., projects and papers), how and when assessment will take place, and the criteria for success. The syllabus describes each task's role in accomplishing the goals and objectives.

The syllabus also presents the timetable for the course, with critical points specified, such as when specific readings are to be done, tests given, and final projects and papers submitted. It is essential that the timeline be on the syllabus, especially when classroom groups are involved, as students need this guidance to break down a major task into smaller tasks with specific due dates. Further, if some groups are working independently, a timeline can keep them focused on the goal.

The syllabus is the major resource for information on expected class behaviors and care should be taken to spell out major categories of behavior that promote learning and enhance grades received. It may be helpful to phrase these expectations in positive rather than negative terms. For example, if attendance is important, points could be given for attendance rather than deducted for absence. Whatever the instructor may want to emphasize should be specified on the syllabus, such as the importance of prompt submission of work (by specifying due dates), the importance of taking tests at the scheduled time (by noting that only rarely and under special circumstances will tests be given after the specified date), or the importance of regular and punctual class attendance (by citing this as a part of professional responsibility). Spelling out expectations on the syllabus is very important when using classroom groups, for the instructor may not be meeting with the class as often or regularly as with a traditional class. Because groups often function independently, much more structure and specificity are needed to better define expected parameters and behavior.

THE STUDENTS

Knowing the general interests, abilities, and personalities of the students can aid an instructor in planning for groups in the course. An important consideration, for example, is if the course is one that majors in the discipline take or one that students from many majors can be expected to enroll in. Students will be more homogeneous if only majors are in the course, and more heterogeneous if from many majors. The instructor would organize the groups and course accordingly in order to be effective. It is not possible or feasible to have all of this information prior to the beginning of the course, but, if the course has been taught previously, some reflection can produce a general description of the students.

Following are examples of some characteristics and their implications in setting up classroom groups. These are but a few and are not all-inclusive. The instructor who intends to use classroom groups can use what is presented or use the basic concepts that fit his or her students. It may be helpful to focus on the students as a group and use a general impression, since every class contains students with a variety of characteristics. All students in a class will not have a specific characteristic, but as a group they will convey an impression. Also important is to consider several or more characteristics and not just one or two. The characteristics are presented as polarities and include:

- Major versus non-major
- Global versus specific perspective
- Extraverted versus introverted preference
- Concepts versus feelings orientation
- Anxious versus relaxed demeanor
- Aggressive versus passive attitude

Major versus Non-Major

Many courses in the major are at the upper level and so major students are usually more focused and motivated about the subject matter. Non-majors are usually taking a course because it is required and may know nothing about the subject or may not be interested. The instructor will have different considerations when setting up group experiences for these two sets of students.

The group for non-majors will need more **"selling"** on the part of the instructor. Students are dealing with ignorance of subject matter, a fear of appearing stupid, and, maybe, some resistance to being forced to take this particular course. The group of majors, on the other hand, are somewhat familiar with the subject matter, and even if they do not want to take the particular course, are less resistant because they accept that this course has to be completed for the major.

In the case of non-majors, an instructor will have to do more explaining of the subject matter and expectations for the group work, as well as provide more support. These students are more likely to need reassurance, specific instructions, and frequent feedback from the instructor. An instructor also needs to be patient with non-majors' confusion, frustration, and intolerance of ambiguity when working in an unfamiliar discipline.

Majors will also need some **"selling,"** particularly if they are unfamiliar with classroom group work. However, they tend to accept the concept of group work more readily, as they have more confidence in the instructor's expertise for structuring their learning experience, and more confidence in their own abilities. In short, students in the major begin with a greater sense of safety and trust, and both conditions promote the group's development.

Global versus Specific Perspective

Some students learn best when they first understand the context, or global perspective, and after that they learn the specifics. Others learn best when the specifics are presented first and later put in context. An instructor usually finds it most effective to present material in ways that are logical, clear, and congruent with the students' learning perspectives, whether global or specific.

When introducing groups into the classroom, it may be even more important to explain the group structure by addressing both these perspectives, especially when students are unfamiliar with groups and how they function. By meeting the needs of students with both global and specific perspectives the instructor promotes safety, trust, and confidence in group process.

An instructor who is introducing the concept of group work to students can meet the global perspective by putting the expectations of the group and its outcomes in context, and tying them to real-world considerations. For example, numerous work situations use teams or groups. Describing some of these situations at the beginning of the course provides some context. It is even more effective when the instructors can cite literature in support, and describe how the classroom group experience mirrors real-life expectations.

The specifics perspective can be addressed through the instructor's structuring of the groups. Students with a specifics perspective need to know before they begin working how the group will work, their role, and the intended learning outcomes. The context is not unimportant, but it is more useful for their understanding after they have incorporated some of the specifics. The instructor can also help specifics-oriented students by having a detailed syllabus and by reviewing requirements during the first few sessions. The more detail an instructor can provide that is clarifying and reasonable, the more this particular perspective will be met.

Some words of caution: It is not sufficient to instruct students to read about group work; the instructor must also present and explain the subject. Neither is it necessary to try to anticipate all questions students may have. Experience can help the instructor focus on the major questions that consistently arise, and then provide answers for these on the syllabus. Lastly, an instructor must be prepared for many questions from students at the beginning of class, when they will be anxious about both the course content and the group structure.

Extraverted versus Introverted Personality

Some majors seem to attract students who tend to be extraverted and some majors attract students who tend to be introverted. Extraverts' orientations and main interests are in the outer world of people and things; they derive their energy from outside themselves. The introvert's orientation is toward the inner world of concepts and ideas. No one person is exclusively introverted or extraverted, but typically there is a preference of one over the other. An introvert can, of course, be social, and an extravert can be reflective.

Meisgeier, Murphy, and Meisgeier (1989) provide the following description in Table 2.1 of extraverted and introverted personality characteristics. A mixture of the two types in a group can be very productive, as they can complement each other. The mixture can also produce conflict and many opportunities for misunderstanding. This is another reason why it is important to know if the course is for majors or a wider audience, as majors tend to be more homogeneous in orientation. For example, students attracted to engineering and to sciences tend to be introverted. However, there may be times when non-majors have to take these courses and some of the non-majors may have a preference for extraversion and the instructor needs to be aware of this characteristic and adapt their instruction such as that described in the next paragraph.

An instructor can consider these characteristics in planning for the group by structuring the activities to satisfy the needs of the dominant type, but also to make accommodations for both. For example, if students tend to be extraverted, the group could be structured to provide:

Table 2.1 Extraverted and Introverted Personality Types and Learning Preferences

Type	Preferences
Extraverted	Tends to prefer variety and action
	Enjoys talking about ideas
	Responsive to people and situations in the environment
	Derives energy from being with others
	Impatient with long, slow projects
Introverted	Concentrates on a few tasks at a time
	Derives energy from ideas
	Needs privacy and time for reflection
	Must understand an idea or project before attempting it
	May not communicate thoughts and feelings

Source: Meisgeier, C., E. Murphy, & C. Meisgeier. (1989). *A teacher's guide to type.* Consulting Pyschologists Press. Palo Alto, CA.

- Time to talk over the problem and get acquainted before beginning work
- Occasional reconsideration of decisions, since extraverts can be somewhat impulsive in making decisions
- Opportunity to watch or try an experiment themselves before it is explained
- Minimal distractions, as extraverts can be easily diverted from tasks

If students tend to be introverted, the group could be structured to provide:

- Time for reflection before requiring action or a decision
- Group leaders who specifically solicit introverted students' input
- Fewer questions that require spontaneous answers
- An emphasis on concepts as well as on fact or simple recall

Concepts versus Feelings Orientation

Some students value concepts over feelings and some value feelings over concepts. Those who value concepts tend to prefer individual work, while those who value feelings tend to enjoy working with others. A focus on concepts describes the student who:

- Wants to know why, not just how
- Dislikes chit-chat
- Enjoys solitary, independent work
- Wants information presented briefly and concisely
- Is analytical and task-oriented

A focus on feelings describes the student who:

- Avoids confrontation and conflict
- Views things from a personal perspective
- Is concerned about relationships and harmony
- Wants to know how the subject affects people
- Has difficulty accepting criticism

An instructor can accommodate each type of student by using many of the following. For concept-oriented students, he or she should:

- Provide logical outlines of information they are expected to know
- Use many instances of problem-solving
- Provide immediate or prompt feedback
- Make sure individual achievement is recognized

For feelings-oriented students, an instructor should:

- Give personal encouragement
- Allow time for group discussion
- Provide incentives for their helping other group members; for example, the group grade could be dependent on how the weakest member of the group performs

Anxious versus Relaxed Demeanor

All students experience some anxiety, especially in new situations, but some students use their anxiety in constructive ways to energize and encourage themselves. These are the students who are excited about new, untried situations; although they are anxious, they are also willing to take some risks and try out new ways of doing and learning.

Other students allow their anxiety to paralyze them so that they cannot perform up to their usual standards. These are the students described as "anxious." The "relaxed" student is not necessarily relaxed, but he or she is more able to contain anxiety and thus perform effectively.

If the students in a class tend to be anxious, the instructor must be patient and reassuring to get the students started and functioning. Anxious students are capable, but they have to be convinced that they will not do something irrevocably fatal before they can proceed. Some may view this as a lack of self-confidence, and such behavior certainly has some elements in common with that characteristic. However, it is much more than a simple lack of confidence, for it permeates their being and affects their behavior. Reassurance, encouragement, and structure help, but these students will remain somewhat anxious no matter what an instructor does or how well they perform—and many do perform very well.

Relaxed students have anxiety that is more readily controlled. They are anxious at the beginning of the class, but are easily reassured that things will be clearer and less confusing as they become more involved in the task. These students are very helpful to their anxious peers. The downside of having many relaxed students, however, is that some may be so "laid-back" that they do not begin the task early enough for maximum effort. In addition, if all or most group members fall into this category, there may be no one to keep the group focused on the task. Relaxed students can procrastinate, sometimes with disastrous results.

Aggressive versus Passive Attitude

Aggressive, in this discussion, describes someone who is forceful, determined, very assertive, strong in viewpoints and opinions, difficult to deflect from a decision, and goal-oriented. Aggression, in this discussion, is *not* dominating, forcing, having one's own way, or exhibiting verbally or physically aggressive behavior. The description used here is more like the high end of assertiveness.

Passive, for purposes of this discussion, describes someone timid, vacillating, unsure or unwilling to make decisions quickly, possessed of many opinions or views on the same topic, tentative, and more relationship- than task-oriented.

If most, or all, students in a class tend to fit the description for *aggressive* the groups will be characterized by conflict, clashes, more independent than collaborative or cooperative work, and accomplishment at the expense of relationships between members. Members are likely to learn to dislike group work and to remain ignorant about how to work productively in a group unless care is taken to instruct them in cooperative group behavior.

If most, or all, students tend to fit the passive profile their groups will be characterized by considerable discussion with little movement toward accomplishing the task. Decisions will be made but constantly revisited and revised. Members will need reassurance from the instructor at every step that they are not making mistakes, and there will be considerable procrastinating. Members will know a great deal about each other, show consideration and respect for others, and be willing to listen to varying opinions and views. These students will leave group work with an understanding of fellow group members and how to cooperate, but little or no grasp of how to accomplish a task while maintaining relationships, unless care is taken to instruct them in how to do so.

An instructor with a class that has both types of students should form mixed groups to capitalize on the strengths of each. Realistically, however, it is difficult to do this unless the instructor has previously worked with these particular students and knows them well enough to make these judgments.

A good method for accommodating each type is to provide specific instructions for how the groups are to function. For example, decisions can be made by consensus rather than by majority, which ensures that a more passive group member is not ignored or discounted. However, the instructions should also provide a schedule for when decisions and work must be final and conveyed to the instructor to avoid products that are constantly revised and never accomplished. Another possible instruction is to require the group leader to actively solicit input from each member, not just throw the floor open. The more tentative members may be reluctant to volunteer an opinion but will do so if requested.

Summary

These are but a few of students' characteristics that impact the effectiveness, productivity, and members' satisfaction with classroom groups. Instructors who actively plan for classroom groups can benefit from reflecting on the general characteristics of students likely to enroll in the course. Knowing the students will help to prevent problems, promote cooperative and collaborative learning, and contribute to more satisfactory group experiences for both the instructor and the students.

GUIDELINES FOR FORMING GROUPS

There are four major considerations when planning to incorporate group work into a class:

- Group size
- Formation of groups
- Directions for how the group is to function
- Physical environment arrangements

Group Size

Five to seven members is a good group size for most projects. This number leaves some room for attrition but is not too large to schedule meetings and promote interaction.

Classroom discussion groups should be small enough, i.e., 5–7 members, so that each member has opportunities to contribute, express an opinion, and provide feedback. Having too many members in the group when trying to complete the task within the constraints of class time can be very frustrating to those who do not get ample opportunity to express their opinions.

Study groups, on the other hand, derive benefit from having more members, as this enlarges the pool of expertise available. Study groups tend to be more informally organized with less emphasis placed on attendance. Thus, having more members can help ensure that a minimum number attend each session. However, the maximum should be 10 members.

Forming Groups

There is no one agreed-upon method for forming groups. However, personal experience with a number of methods and the experience of instructors in many disciplines leads to the recommendation that the instructor form groups by:

- Deciding the number of groups that can be formed
- Establishing the minimum number of members for each group
- Assigning students to groups by having them count off in a predetermined sequence; all students with the same number are in the same group

For example, if there are 21 students in the class an instructor could choose to have three or four groups, assuming a minimum group size of five (i.e., three groups of 7 members each or three groups of 5 members and one group with 6 members). If the goal is to have three groups, have students repeatedly count off 1, 2, 3; all 1's will form a group, and so on. This usually produces a good mix of abilities and characteristics, and has the advantage of being a somewhat random method of assignment. This technique is especially effective in randomizing group assignments when the instructor does not start the count at a corner of the room. Try using a spiral counting-off procedure, beginning at any position. Using a spiral procedure and beginning the count from the middle of the room or of a row together reduce the likelihood of having a group, or groups, of friends and increase the likelihood of heterogeneity in the groups.

It is not wise to let students select their own groups. When students are allowed to form their own groups they naturally gravitate to familiar faces. Any student who is not known or not a member of a social circle may not be invited to participate in any group. Thus, from the beginning of the group experience, some members feel included and some excluded. The excluded student who is assigned late to a group by the instructor begins his or her group experience:

- Having to deal with a set of members who have bonded because they know each other
- Feeling forced on the group by the instructor
- Being a "stranger"

None of this is in the open or addressed by the group, but it will affect the functioning of the group and how members feel about the group, especially the unknown student.

Another danger in letting students select their own groups is that already existing friendships between members will evolve into a "clique." A clique can destroy trust in a group, as members of a clique will tend to support and listen to each other and shut off input from other members. In so doing, they impose the ideas, opinions, and decisions of the "clique" rather than arriving at a decision by consensus, or using ideas and input from all members. Again, those not in the clique will feel, and be, excluded. Further, friends may tend to talk about group matters and members outside the classroom. One cannot prevent this from happening, but group members who do not have preexisting relationships are less likely to have these potentially inappropriate discussions.

Exclusion of group members for any reason does not foster group development. The following example illustrates the negative effect of letting students select their groups and the instructor then having to assign "strangers."

Most classes in engineering are composed of males, and in predominantly white universities, most of the males are also white. There are some minorities and women, but very few in any given class. An instructor who uses self-selection for groups will most likely have to assign the women and minority students. All too often what happens is that the majority of group members will then hold impromptu or even scheduled meetings at their convenience and in places that may not be suitable for all members. Examples of unsuitable meeting times would be late at night or early morning, for example 1 A.M., or on the weekend for commuter students who may be off campus or have to work at those times. Examples of unsuitable meeting places are bars, unsupervised facilities, and men's bathrooms. If instructors must use the self-selection method for groups, they have to be careful to specify when and where meetings can be held outside the classroom, and to make sure all members can be accommodated so that any "strangers" will not be consciously or unconsciously excluded by their inability to attend impromptu meetings or meetings held in unsafe or inappropriate places.

This is not an extreme example of what can happen when students select their groups and "strangers" are assigned. It is a more vivid illustration when "strangers" are women and minorities in a predominantly white male environment, but the same principle holds for other groups. For example, when the majority are female they may exclude males; or when the majority are black they may exclude white students. Much or most of this exclusion may not be deliberate, but the alert instructor can prevent it from happening by forming groups more randomly and specifying where and when meetings can and cannot be held.

The final argument against letting students select their groups is that they will not be able to choose their work group, or team, when they enter the world of work. They can expect to be assigned to a group and to have to learn to work cooperatively within that group. They will be evaluated on how well they mesh with other members, the group's productivity, and their individual effort. All of these conditions should be mirrored in their classroom group. An instructor will find it more beneficial to state this rationale for forming groups at the beginning and to resist any and all arguments for letting students choose their groups.

Group Directions and Guidelines

The directions for how groups will function should be clearly stated on the syllabus. The syllabus is part of the instructor's contract with students and must specify conditions for participation, outcomes, and evaluation. The written directions can also serve as references for students who may have questions throughout the class. No matter how carefully the instructions are written, an instructor should also orally review them at the beginning of the class, emphasizing the most significant ones.

The basic directions for how the group will function can include the following:

- Meetings
- Decisions
- Meeting minutes
- Task assignments
- Participation requirements
- Conflicts

Each of these is briefly described in the following discussion.

Meetings

An important point to specify and emphasize is that formal group meetings will have to meet the instructor's standards and approval. The instructor should explicitly state that meetings must be held at times and places where all members can attend and that impromptu meetings of only some members are prohibited. Meetings cannot be held in bars or other places where alcohol is available or in places that are unsafe or threatening for any group member. It is also preferable that group meetings be held on campus and at times when commuters can attend. One method to accomplish this is to have each group set up a schedule at the beginning of the course for approval by the instructor. Conditions for students may change, such as job or family responsibilities, necessitating changes in the group's meeting time or place, but the instructor can provide for these changes by specifying that all changes must be approved in advance of the meeting. This one direction vastly reduces impromptu and exclusionary changes in group meetings. Knowing that the instructor is paying attention and considers group protocol important carries a lot of weight with the students.

Decisions

An instructor should emphasize that decisions are to be made by consensus, for the most part, and not by majority voting. It is important to have this specified in the directions and reviewed by the instructor. While it may not always be possible to avoid having decisions by majority rule, students should be encouraged to employ consensual decision making because it solicits input from all members and results in all members helping to carry out the decision because they were a part of it. In consensus, there are not winners and losers, as in other forms of decision making.

Meeting Minutes

Another important aspect of group functioning is the necessity of communicating transactions to the instructor, preferably in the form of written minutes. The instructor needs to monitor what is happening in each group and minutes can expedite this monitoring and help the instructor to know when intervention may be needed to keep the group on the right track. It is recommended that groups submit minutes of meetings and that these minutes note decisions made. Minutes should be brief, noting attendees and absentees; day, time, and place of meeting; major topics discussed; tasks assigned and persons responsible; and decisions made. These minutes can be as brief as one page but should be submitted to the instructor within seven days after the meeting. An instructor may want to make submission of minutes a part of the grade for the group. This can insure compliance and reward diligence and attention to responsibility.

Task Assignments

An instructor also needs to know from the beginning how the group has divided the work and who is responsible for each task. Students may not have enough knowledge about the extent of time and effort needed to accomplish each task at the beginning of the class and this ignorance can lead to an unequal division of labor that can become difficult to correct later. If the instructor provides a list of tasks, then the group has only to decide each member's responsibility. If, however, learning how to conceptualize a project and break it down into smaller tasks is a part of the course, the group should both divide the work and assign responsibility. In either case, these are a part of directions for group functioning. An instructor can ask for the list of task assignments and responsibilities as a separate submission due within the first two weeks and subject to instructor approval, or as continuing information in the minutes. Both methods allow for instructor monitoring and intervention. Depending on the project and extent of tasks, using one or both of these methods can also permit the instructor to assign individual grades.

Participation Requirements

If groups function ideally, all group members will actively participate. However, ideal conditions seldom exist. Further, some students may not fully understand what participation means in terms of behavior. It may seem elementary to an instructor, but specifying in behavioral terms what participation means reduces ambiguity and promotes students' feelings of security that they are meeting the instructor's expectations. Basic directions for active participation include:

- Attending all group meetings and class sessions on time
- Providing input
- Helping to make decisions
- Carrying out task assignments

Some students are not inclined to take group meetings seriously and consider them a waste of time. They prefer to work independently and feel that they can work better that way. These are the students who resist group work by being absent and/or tardy. The instructor can reduce or eliminate this behavior and emphasize the importance of group work by specifying attendance goals and by either awarding points for attendance or decreasing points for absence. I usually set it up so that one or two latenesses or absences will not usually depress the final grade, but more than that will have a negative impact. After all, students can have unanticipated crises or illnesses, and need a little leeway.

Other aspects of participation that can be specified and highlighted are:

- Providing input, both voluntarily and when solicited
- Participating in discussions to make decisions
- Giving opinions
- Voicing any concerns
- Responding directly to other group members' input

All these behaviors enhance group functioning. The leader does not have sole responsibility for the group's functioning; if members engage in active participation, the group will work well.

Conflicts

Many students may resist or fear having to work in groups because they dread conflicts or dealing with conflicts. It is not possible, however, to have a conflict-free group. Conflicts are a part of every relationship and of every group. But it is possible to learn how to constructively manage and resolve conflicts, as well as one's own behavior in and reaction to conflicts. Constructive conflict management is discussed more extensively in Chapter 6; addressed here is the need for an instructor to provide directions to the group for communicating disruptive and unresolved conflicts to the instructor in a timely manner. All too often, conflicts in classroom groups are left to fester until it becomes almost impossible to have an agreeable resolution. Many times an instructor does not have any clue about the conflict, the extent or depth of feelings aroused, and the fragility of the group, because members do not solicit the instructor's help. The instructor is left with the toxic fallout, which is almost impossible to overcome. This is another reason why it is important to have directions for groups about conflicts.

A skilled group leader can be very effective in constructive conflict resolution. However, since many, or most, student group leaders or facilitators will not have prior preparation in conflict resolution or mediation, it may be difficult for them to focus on both accomplishing the task and learning a new skill. An instructor can help by making it clear that he or she is to be considered a member of the group and kept informed about conflicts and concerns. Group leaders will meet regularly with the instructor and at those meetings conflicts can be reported and suggestions for resolution provided. Further, each group member should feel free to contact the instructor through e-mail or other means. It may be helpful for an instructor to emphasize that conflicts can be more constructively resolved if they are brought out in the group instead of internalized, and steps taken to mediate or resolve them. Further, an instructor should be prepared to intervene to keep conflicts from escalating and destroying the group, which can and does happen.

Physical Environment Arrangements

This discussion is limited to what the instructor can realistically provide in the classroom or in related facilities (e.g., lab rooms) during class time. Not all group meetings may be held under these same circumstances. However, an instructor can suggest that the group leader try to use at least similar arrangements.

Why pay attention to physical environment? Because some simple arranging of the environment can help facilitate communication among members, reduce or eliminate intrusions, and promote feelings of safety. The three major aspects of arranging the physical environment are seating arrangements for visual and auditory contact, privacy, and accessibility to the instructor. Even the most uninviting classroom can be arranged to help achieve these needs.

Seating Arrangements

Seating arrangements for visual and auditory contact allow each group member to readily see every other group member. This may appear to be somewhat elementary, but it can be easily overlooked. All too often one or more group members are seated at an angle or even outside the group, making it impossible for them to maintain visual and auditory contact with each member and vice versa. It is difficult to feel or be a part of a group, when one cannot see facial expressions or hear everything that is said, or when one is facing someone's back.

An instructor should either personally arrange the seating or direct students to do so. If the second option is chosen, care must be taken to make sure students arrange the seating so that all group members are included. If chairs are movable, a circular seating arrangement is best. Circles must be large enough to include all members, and students must not be allowed to elect to sit outside the circle. If tables and chairs are available, then seating can be arranged around the table(s). More difficult to arrange is seating with fixed chairs, such as in an auditorium. Sometimes, the seats swivel and a quasi-circle can be formed. It may be best just to find other group meeting places if chairs are fixed.

Privacy

Small groups should be sufficiently distant from each other so that noise can be controlled and some measure of privacy implemented. Noise and intrusion control is very important, as both can be irritating and disruptive. Ideally, each group will have a separate meeting room in proximity to the classroom so that an instructor can easily move between groups and be accessible for consultation.

One aid to establishing safety and trust in a group is an assurance that what is discussed in the group will be kept confidential. Members need to feel free to express ideas and opinions, or even to make personal disclosures without fearing that they will be overheard or talked about outside the group. Privacy for group meetings can facilitate this to some extent. Complete confidentiality cannot be maintained in a group, however, and, as was discussed earlier, some things must and will be reported to the instructor since he or she is a member of every group.

Observation and Monitoring
It is important for the first few meetings that the instructor have ready access to every group in order to monitor how the group is functioning, provide input on the task and how it can be accomplished, identify potential problems, and give students support and encouragement. This is especially crucial if students are unfamiliar with working in groups or are resistant to group work.

The instructor can accomplish these aims when groups are physically located so that some time can be spent with each group as an observer. The instructor should make it clear in advance that this is what will happen so that students are not surprised or taken aback when he or she walks in the room or sits nearby to hear what is going on.

THE FIRST GROUP MEETING: GETTING UNDER WAY

Classroom groups benefit from instructor-provided direction and structure in the beginning stages. It is not easy to know what level of direction and structure is sufficient to get the group started, provide safety and trust, reduce confusion, and promote student confidence. Even experienced instructors of groups can find it difficult to give too little or too much direction and structure, because each class is sufficiently different that one cannot accurately predict what will be needed. So many times it seems that one is accurate by chance and not by virtue of knowledge and experience.

Basic course directions and structure patterns are set by the syllabus and by how the instructor oversees and organizes the early group meetings. The first group meeting should be held during the first class meeting. It can be brief, 15 to 20 minutes, but students will better understand the group's role and importance if an instructor makes it a part of the course from the outset.

Introduction of Group Work

Group work can be introduced during the review of the syllabus. The relative importance of the group, how participation and outcomes will be evaluated, and minimum expectations for students should be on the syllabus. The instructor can elaborate on the importance of the group by providing an oral rationale during the review. For example, the instructor might say, "Group work is intended to introduce students to working cooperatively and collaboratively"; or, "Using groups mirrors what students will encounter when they enter their careers"; or, "Recent surveys of alumni and their employers have highlighted the need for students to learn how to work in groups." However an instructor chooses to introduce group work, its importance must be emphasized, as many students tend to focus more on cognitive tasks, especially if they are unfamiliar with or resistant to group work. Other specifics that can be introduced are how, when, and where group meetings are to be held; evaluation of the leader, group members, and the group work; and how individual effort as well as group effort will be evaluated.

Determination of the Group Leader

Prior to the beginning of class an instructor must make a decision about how the group leaders will be designated. Will they be selected by the instructor, be elected by group members, volunteer, be allowed to emerge, or rotate leadership with others, as is described in Chapter 5? Each of these ways has advantages and disadvantages. The important piece at this point is that the instructor make the form of leader designation part of the course directions. Students also need to know what the responsibilities of the group leader are and how these leaders will be prepared for leadership. It is recommended that an instructor meet weekly with group leaders during the first few weeks of the course to monitor the group, help structure group meetings, and support, reassure, and encourage group leaders. Group members will feel safer if they know that the instructor is helping to direct meetings even when absent, has some knowledge of what is transpiring, and cares about the members and progress of the group. The extent of students' unexpressed anxieties cannot be overestimated.

Designation of the Group Recorder

The other role that must be assigned is that of the recorder, who will take the minutes and relay them to other members and the instructor. The instructor can choose to let someone volunteer, allow group members to decide if they want to assign one person as recorder or rotate the responsibility, or mandate that each group member will serve as recorder at least once or twice during the course. It may be least frustrating for the instructor, however, to make this job a fixed role with some incentive, such as points toward the grade, attached. The recorder is an important role, involving time and effort that should be rewarded in some way.

Structure of the First Group Session

Since the group's first meeting will be an abbreviated session, probably with much student confusion, tasks for the first session should be structured and planned in advance by the instructor. The following is suggested as a guide for the first session:

- Ice-breaker or get-acquainted exercise
- Group goal-setting
- Exchange of e-mail, mail address, phone, and fax numbers

Even when group members know each other, it is important and helpful to have an ice-breaker or get-acquainted exercise. Students will tend to want to jump directly to the task because it is easier than tending to relationship issues. However, relationship issues are more important in the beginning than are task issues. Further, the task is still ambiguous and not fully understood.

Following are examples for ice-breakers and get-acquainted exercises. These are easy to do, require little preparation, and help students to begin to get to know each other.

Ice-Breaker and Get-Acquainted Exercises
Get-acquainted and ice-breaker exercises are simple, easy to do for someone who is unfamiliar with exercises and games, and do not take much time. They are intended to make the transition to the group smoother, help members begin to know and communicate with each other, and reduce anxieties about the group. Following are three such exercises. The instructor may want to collect the index cards after the groups meet and review them, both to make sure directions were followed and to get to know students in the class.

Ice Breaker #1, My Ideal Career

- Materials: index cards, pens or pencils, list of characteristics posted at the front of the room
- Time: 10 minutes
- Procedure: Prepare the following list of career characteristics and post where all students can see them.

My ideal career will allow me to:

Have power

Achieve status, prestige

Make considerable money

Discover something new

Invent things or develop processes

Have a lot of fun

Take frequent vacations

Retire early

Do satisfying tasks

Find a better way to do things, care for people, etc.

Distribute materials to students. Tell them they have 10 minutes to accomplish this exercise. Direct students to list three to five career characteristics they consider personally important on one side of the card. Then have them fold the card in half lengthwise and write their name and nickname on one side. After dividing students into groups, tell students to find similarities among group members for their choices of career characteristics and to place the folded cards in front of them as name cards so group members can begin to learn each other's names.

Ice Breaker #2, My Strengths

- Materials: index cards, pens or pencils
- Time: 10 minutes
- Procedure: Distribute materials to students. Tell them they have 10 minutes to complete the exercise. Introduce the exercise by noting that each person has strengths or weaknesses and that it is important to focus on strengths and capitalize on them rather than having most or all of the attention given to remediating weaknesses. Further note that each student brings some strengths and expertise to the group. Then have students list their names and three to five personal strengths on their cards. Examples of strengths are:

Good time management

Computer graphics skills

Ability to get along with nearly everyone

Keen sense of curiosity

Love of learning

Library research skills

Writing talent

Computing ability

Organizing skills

- Instruct students to share their lists after breaking them into their small groups.

Ice Breaker #3, Some of My Favorite Things

- Materials: index cards, pens or pencils
- Time: 10–15 minutes
- Procedure: Distribute materials to the students. Tell them they have 15 minutes for the task. Introduce the exercise by noting that people who work effectively in groups or teams find that they have many similarities in values, attitudes, beliefs, personality, likes, dislikes, and so on. While they also have some differences, they tend to be more alike than different. This exercise helps to begin the process of finding similarities among group members. Have students then respond to the following or other instructor-developed open-ended questions.

My favorite color(s) are _____.

Three things I do well are _____.

My favorite TV shows are _____.

Three things I like to do are _____.

One thing that annoys me is _____.

My favorite time of the year is _____.

- Students share their answers after breaking into their small groups and try to identify similarities among themselves.

Four additional resources for get-acquainted/ice-breaker exercises are *Group Structured Exercises* by Pheiffer and Jones, with new volumes published each year since 1970 and are now available including back issues, from Jossey-Bass; *More Games Trainers Play* by Scannell and Newsome (1983); *Expressive Processes in Group Counseling* (Brown, 1996); and *Psychoeducational Groups* (Brown, 1998).

Group Goal-Setting
It is important to have students focusing on goals from the very beginning, which makes goal-setting a recommended task for the first group meeting. There are two basic methods: Groups can be instructed to develop goals, or the instructor can prepare a list of possible cognitive and group goals and instruct groups to discuss them, select the two or three that seem most important, and add others if they want. An effective process is to first have all students in the class develop a list of personal goals, then divide students into groups and have them share these goals, and next have them develop group

goals consistent with individual goals. After the first group meeting of 15 to 20 minutes during class time, the class reconvenes and each group reports its goals.

When students become a part of developing goals for their learning they are more likely to try and achieve them. This is especially true when some effort is made to incorporate their individual goals into the course and group goals.

One important note to the instructor: Try to be accepting of the goals developed by students. It can be disheartening to hear that some students' goals only relate to the grades they want, but it is important that the instructor not throw cold water at this point. All the students in the class are waiting to see if it will be safe to express honest opinions in this class and if the instructor is interested in them. In a case in which a student's goal was a grade in the course, the instructor could promote feelings of trust and safety by responding neutrally with something like, "Grades can be very important."

Exchange of Contact Information

The final task for the first group meeting is to have members exchange information on how best to reach them when out of class, including mailing address, e-mail address, home and work telephone, and fax number. These should be summarized on one sheet, with a copy given to each member and the instructor. These sheets can be very handy for members to communicate with each other and especially helpful for the instructor.

SUMMARY

The instructor who intends to use group work in a course has considerable planning and work to do prior to the first class. Groups will run more effectively if an instructor pays attention to the basic concerns discussed in this chapter. The next few chapters will elaborate further on some topics introduced in this chapter, such as the syllabus, goals and objectives, contracts, the first few group meetings, and strategies for evaluating groups.

CHAPTER 3

Organizing and Guiding

THE ROLE OF THE SYLLABUS

The most valuable tool for an instructor in organizing a course and guiding students is a syllabus that covers the essentials expected of students. A syllabus should give students basic information about:

- Expectations for behavior and learning
- Prior knowledge necessary for success
- How and when evaluation will take place
- The schedule of readings, assignments, and tests
- The relative importance of various class activities

Syllabi that also provide guidelines for performance, such as projects and term papers, are more effective than those that do not. An instructor should not rely on verbal communication for conveying guidelines and directions, as some students are not always present in the classroom when these are presented, and others will not hear them correctly. Written guidelines reduce (though they will not eliminate) the need to repeat this information.

There will always be some students who do not read or refer to the syllabus. However, these are the minority; the majority of students appreciate a well-constructed extensive syllabus.

Most, if not all, colleges and universities, as well as their professional schools, undergo some sort of accreditation process. Accrediting bodies generally have specific guidelines for syllabi. Various accrediting agencies agree on the basic components of a syllabus; these are briefly discussed below, along with other syllabus components that assume particular importance in courses using classroom groups. A suggested syllabus outline is presented in Table 3.1.

Table 3.1 Suggested Syllabus Outline

Course title	Instructor name
Course number	Office # and location
Catalogue description	Fax #
Days and times class meets	Phone #
Location of class/labs	e-mail address
Goals and objectives	Scheduled office hours
Prerequisites	Teaching assistant data
Attendance requirements	Texts and other required supplies and equipment
Honor code	Course-specific requirements
Accommodation of special needs	Grading scheme
Course requirements	Tests, assignments, and reading schedule

Basic Syllabus Information

Identifying Data

It may seem redundant and simplistic to have the course title, number, catalog description, and scheduled class meeting days and time on a syllabus, but this is basic orienting information. After some personal experiences with students finding out in the second, third, or fourth class session that they are in the wrong class or section, I started the practice of announcing the class title and number at the beginning of the first session and making sure it is on the syllabus in bold letters. Attending the wrong class is not limited to entering freshmen—all students can make that mistake.

Catalog Description

The catalog description is a capsule of course content; by putting it on the syllabus, one highlights what is to be learned. Too many catalog descriptions do not reflect course content, and this discrepancy can be confusing to the conscientious student and adviser who read the catalog and use it for guidance. An instructor needs to be alert to the fit between planned course content and the catalog description and try to make them congruent or, when the time rolls around, change the catalog description. Accrediting bodies do examine syllabi for these congruencies, for the catalog is considered to be the university or college contract with students.

Instructor Information

Also very basic is the instructor's name; office number and location; phone and fax numbers; e-mail address; scheduled office hours for availability to students; and, if there are teaching or graduate assistants, their names, locations, hours of availability, and phone, fax, and e-mail information. Why provide so much detail? One important reason is that knowing when and how to reach the instructor gives students some assurance that the "expert consultant" will be available to clarify, answer questions, resolve an impasse or conflict, and so on. This reassurance contributes to feelings of safety and confidence that students, especially those students working in groups, will not be cast adrift or allowed to flounder. This reassurance is very important at the beginning of class and, while the need lessens as time goes on, it never completely goes away.

It is not sufficient to announce this information in class, post it on the office door, or tell students to ask the department secretary or graduate assistants; the information should also be written on the syllabus. Do not overlook information about graduate or teaching assistants, as they are frequently given responsibility for significant parts of a class, and students will also need to consult with them.

Major Course Policies
Much of the information in this section will be derived from the individual college or university's policies. Instructors should consult the catalogue and faculty handbook at their institutions on policies on class attendance, honor code and system, and accommodation for students with special needs and disabilities. If the instructor is required, or chooses, to enforce the honor system and accommodate special needs, then this should be stated on the syllabus. Simple statements such as those in the examples below should be sufficient.

Honor Code
"I pledge to support the honor code of _____. I will refrain from any form of academic dishonesty or deception, such as cheating or plagiarism. I am aware that as a member of the academic community, it is my responsibility to turn in all suspected violators of the honor code. I will report to an Honor Council hearing if summoned."

Accommodating Special Needs
In accordance with university policy, students with documented sensory and/or learning disabilities should inform the instructor so that their special needs may be accommodated.

Attendance
Class attendance policies vary by institution and many leave the decision to the instructor, although a policy can state that instructor may require attendance and that grades can be dependent on attendance. In these instances, an instructor must state what the attendance policy is for the particular class.

If grades are not affected by absences, then it may not be necessary to state an attendance policy on the syllabus.

It is important to have a written attendance policy for group meetings on the syllabus. An instructor should also specify how attendance will impact grades; for example, missing two or more sessions will result in the individual's grade for the group being reduced a certain number of points.

Special Class Policies

Some instructors may have special policies for their classes and these are also a part of the syllabus. For example, I do not permit eating and drinking in my classes and state so on my syllabus. Other classes, such as computer labs, may also have posted policies against food and drink, but even if there are signs, the policy should also be on the syllabus. An instructor can rely on previous experiences to determine what can and cannot be done in class. I have seen syllabi that:

- Prohibited bringing children and pets to class
- Noted that recording lectures was or was not permitted
- Prohibited personal radios or other such devices
- Explained whether the instructor did or did not give makeup tests
- Required prior notification for excused absences
- Described what documentation was needed for an absence to be excused by the instructor

Students seem to operate on a principle that whatever is not prohibited is allowed.

Course Overview

The overview for the course should include:

- A brief list of prerequisite courses, skills, and knowledge
- Course goals and objectives
- Required and optional textbooks and other materials that students must purchase
- Major requirements and their due dates, such as papers and tests and their contributions to the final grade
- Requirements for participation
- The overall grading scheme

Specific guidelines for papers, projects, and groups are not included at this point if you need more than a short paragraph to present these instructions. This course overview should be brief so students can easily see the major course requirements and gauge the effort needed.

Prerequisites

There may be specific prerequisites or co-requisites for the course stated in the catalog, and these should be on the syllabus. Sometimes students and/or advisers fail to note or ignore prerequisites, resulting in students enrolling in classes for which they are not prepared. Students are especially prone to do this as they do not know, or dismiss, the value of prerequisites. Indicating what is expected to be known prior to beginning the class sends a clear message that the instructor intends to begin instruction at a particular point. It also gives students an opportunity to select a more appropriate course.

Goals and Objectives

Goals and major objectives for the course also help orient the students to what is important for them to learn in the course. This is where the instructor can introduce the importance of working in groups, by stating an objective that focuses on the group. It is suggested that there be one goal for the course and a maximum of eight to ten objectives. A guide for developing behavioral objectives is presented later in this chapter.

Required and Optional Materials

All required and optional purchased books and materials are highlighted by placing this information in proximity to the goal and objectives. Other readings can be listed later in the syllabus. This list of required and optional materials informs students of what basic resources are needed for minimal work in the course. It is also helpful to note where these can be obtained, especially if they are not available in the campus bookstore.

Major Course Requirements

A very helpful part of the course overview is a listing and brief description of major course requirements and the associated proportion of the grade. This is where an instructor can highlight the relative importance of each part of the course, especially the group part. It does not hurt to be somewhat redundant and state this in more than one place on the syllabus. An example for stating major requirements is presented in Table 3.2.

Requirement for Participation

When groups are used as part of a course it is helpful to define what the instructor means by participation and to set minimum standards. Just forming groups and expecting students to work is not sufficient. Further, when part of their grade is dependent on participation, students need to know what behaviors and attitudes constitute participation. This can be specified on the syllabus and as part of the separate group work guidelines.

Table 3.2 Examples of Major Requirements in a Class Incorporating Groups

Requirement	Percent of Grade
1. Project	60%
• Written plan	35% of project grade
• Oral presentation	30% of project grade
• Group participation	35% of project grade

Students will form teams to develop a plan for addressing an identified community problem. The plan will include background information, resources needed, available resources, and anticipated outcomes. The plan will be presented in both written and oral formats. The written plan will be composed of individual reports, and each group member is expected to present a part of the oral report. The final grade will be awarded on both individual and group effort. Specific instructions and guidelines for the written plan, oral presentation, and group participation are attached to the syllabus. The final report is due _____.

2. Tests	30 percent

Two tests and a final on lectures, readings, and class discussions will be administered. Makeup tests are discouraged and will be given only if the instructor is notified in advance and approves the absence.

3. Professionalism	10 percent

Students will be evaluated on the degree to which they exhibit professional behavior in the class. Professionalism is defined as those characteristics and behaviors expected by career professionals in the field.

Some behaviors and attitudes that can be used as minimum criteria for participation are attending all scheduled group meetings, being on time, volunteering for and accepting assigned tasks, completing tasks on time, and voicing ideas and opinions. If an instructor uses these behaviors to form the rating scale for group participation, then they should be emphasized on the syllabus. Noting the allowed number of absences and lateness can also be a part of this section.

This section should stress the importance of the group sessions as part of the class to emphasize the role of group work in both learning and the resulting grade. Students are more likely to take group work seriously when they understand from the beginning that the instructor means business.

Overall Grading Scheme

The final part of the course overview is the grading plan or scheme. Although some of this information was presented under major requirements, a review in a separate section can be useful. A sample follows.

Grading Plan

Project	60 percent
3 tests	30 percent
Professionalism	10 percent

Course Specifics

Courses vary considerably in requirements, and instructors must tailor this section for their particular course. "Specifics" refers to activities such as laboratory and computer use, the schedule for readings, assignments, tests, and other work.

It can be helpful to provide students with a weekly schedule for topics to be presented, chapters to read, homework to be completed, due dates for handing in assignments, and test dates. The entire semester's or quarter's specific work can be presented in this section. This schedule allows students to better plan how to accomplish all their required tasks and manage their time.

Task Guidelines

Both students and instructor benefit when written guidelines for the completion of tasks and the basis for grading them are a part of the syllabus. Writing guidelines forces an instructor to describe clearly and simply the specific requirements for the course. This also gives an instructor an opportunity to explain the grading system used. For example, the written plan for a project will be graded on two major areas: content and format. The sample rating scale in Table 3.3 was used for the written part of required feedback reports in my group counseling class. The content portion focuses on criteria discussed in class and in the text on how to provide constructive feedback. The format part focuses on the style and quality of the written material and use of the professional format of the American Psychological Association. This scale makes it easier for students to understand what was done well and what was inadequate or poor. The guidelines for completing the feedback reports clearly state that the reports will be graded on content (how well the reports meet the criteria for constructive feedback) and on format (quantity and quality of writing).

Guidelines for Groups

Guidelines for groups should include the following minimal directions for students:

- Meetings must be held when all members are able to attend.
- Meetings must be held on university premises or at locations approved in advance by the instructor.
- Minutes must be recorded and submitted to the instructor no later than one week after the meeting.
- Leaders will meet at regularly scheduled times with the instructor.
- No racial, sexual, or other forms of harassment will be tolerated.

Table 3.3 Feedback Report Evaluation

Name _____ Date _____ Grade _____

Rating scale

5 excellent, 4 good, 3 adequate, 2 fair, 1 poor, 0 missing

Constructiveness of Feedback

1.	Descriptive rather than evaluative	5	4	3	2	1	0
2.	Specific rather than general	5	4	3	2	1	0
3.	Focused on behavior	5	4	3	2	1	0
4.	Shared information, not advice	5	4	3	2	1	0
5.	Took receiver needs into account	5	4	3	2	1	0
6.	Concerned about what, not why	5	4	3	2	1	0
7.	Thoughtful, not superficial	5	4	3	2	1	0

Preparation

8.	Quality of writing	5	4	3	2	1	0
9.	Quality of presentation	5	4	3	2	1	0
10.	Amount of information	5	4	3	2	1	0
11.	Focused on significant aspects	5	4	3	2	1	0
12.	Reflective of time and effort	5	4	3	2	1	0
13.	Insightful	5	4	3	2	1	0
14.	Showed a high level of awareness	5	4	3	2	1	0

Required Components

15.	Communication skills	5	4	3	2	1	0
16.	Relationship skills	5	4	3	2	1	0
17.	Personal qualities	5	4	3	2	1	0
18.	Awareness of potential countertransference issues	5	4	3	2	1	0

- Accommodations must be made for those with special needs, such as access for wheelchairs.
- Group members are expected to attend every meeting promptly.
- The instructor is considered a member of every group and must be kept informed of actions and events.

Instructors may have additional conditions for groups in their classes. These minimal standards can expedite the functioning of the group and prevent problems. A rationale for most of the guidelines was presented in Chapter 2. An example of phrasing for each direction is given below.

Meeting Times

Each group will develop a schedule for a regular weekly meeting time and provide each member and the instructor with the schedule. The group is expected to select a time when all members can and agree to attend. Unscheduled meetings and impromptu meetings that do not include all group members are prohibited. Group meeting times must be approved in advance by the instructor.

Meeting Location

All meetings will be held on university premises *or* at a location approved in advance by the instructor. No location where alcohol is served will be approved. (Note: This sends a message that alcohol should not be served even if they meet in someone's home, and helps protect both underage students and the instructor.) Meeting places must accommodate any group member with documented special needs.

Minutes

Minutes for each meeting will be submitted to the instructor no later than one week after the meeting is held. Earlier submission is encouraged. Group members may choose to rotate the task of recording and submitting minutes, or have a designated recorder. Minutes are to be one typewritten page with the following required information: names of attendees; names of absentees; leader and recorder identified; meeting date, time, and location; major topics discussed; and any decisions and assignments made.

Group Leaders

Group leaders will schedule regular meetings with the instructor. These will usually be meetings for all group leaders but individual meetings can also be scheduled. Weekly group leader meetings will be held for the first six weeks and biweekly meetings held for the remainder of the course. These meetings will allow the instructor to know what groups are doing, learn of problems encountered or identify potential problems, provide opportunities for teaching leadership skills, and monitor progress toward goal accomplishment.

University Policies

Students are advised to read the catalogue and student handbook on policies relevant to racial and sexual harassment and to act in accordance with these policies. Verbal and/or physical violations will not be tolerated and all reported violations or concerns will be investigated. Any student found to have racially, sexually, or in any other way harassed another student may be removed from the group and the course, and reported to the university authorities.

Participation
Productive groups are characterized by input and effort of all members. Therefore, it is extremely important that every member attend each meeting and participate.

Members will be graded on participation, including attending meetings at the designated time. Missing one or two meetings will not usually have a significant impact on a student's grade. However, missing more than two meetings will result in a lowered grade for participation.

Students must read the guidelines for participation and are encouraged to practice these behaviors and skills, as they characterize an effective and productive group member. (Note: An instructor can develop more specific guidelines for participation from material in Chapter 4.)

Roles of the Instructor and Group Leader
The instructor is a member of every group and must be kept fully informed about the group. All concerns, conflicts, harassment, and other problems must be promptly brought to the instructor's attention. As a group member and consultant, the group leader has the responsibility to monitor and evaluate groups and their members.

Electronically Linked Groups
It is possible, and may be feasible, to allow groups to hold electronically linked meetings. The computer allows for e-mail, bulletin boards, and other computer-accessed meetings. There are several advantages to electronically linked student meetings:

- Members can be anywhere geographically when a meeting is held, as they only need to have access to an appropriate computer or terminal.
- Participation is more equalized.
- Participation is less affected by status and prestige of members.
- Meeting times can be easier to arrange.
- Travel time is reduced or eliminated.

Electronically linked groups are the topic of Chapter 12.

THE ROLE OF THE INSTRUCTOR

Every instructor has several roles, regardless of the course: educator, judge, lecturer, and leader are just a few examples. Each role plays an important part in the success of the class and learning that occurs. The instructor who uses classroom groups takes on even more roles, such as mediator and consultant.

In nearly every classroom, instructors;

- Organize and present information
- Structure tasks and assignments
- Evaluate learning
- Judge the quality of student work

Using classroom groups involves additional tasks of:

- Modeling leadership behaviors and attitudes
- Mediating conflicts
- Developing leadership skills among student leaders
- Observing and managing the groups
- Consulting to the group

An instructor cannot adopt a hands-off position and expect groups to function well on their own without guidance. Further, students have a right to expect that the instructor will know what is happening in the group in order to provide sufficient safety for members. Work for the instructor is increased when using classroom groups, not decreased. Following is a brief description of the additional roles typically assumed by instructors implementing group work and why they are important for an instructor in organizing and guiding a class.

Modeling

One way to learn skills is by observation. Seeing how someone behaves and the impact of that behavior provides a basis for adopting new behaviors and eliminating existing behaviors in the observer. Students are more likely to learn leadership skills when they can observe the instructor actually enacting what he or she is teaching. Instructors should bear in mind that all students in the class are potential group leaders, not just the few currently designated as small group leaders. A list and description of leadership skills is provided in Chapter 10.

Mediating Conflicts

An instructor can expect to mediate some conflicts, for student group leaders may have neither the required expertise nor the authority to handle some conflicts. There may also be some conflicts, such as harassment, that require use of "official" authority. In this case, the instructor is the one who can best intervene; the student leader's responsibility is simply to report the offense to the instructor. Other conflicts, such as lack of responsibility by a member, may also require mediation by an instructor. Mediation and conflict resolution are addressed in Chapter 6.

Developing Student Leaders' Skills

Leadership skills must be taught and nurtured. These are not usually naturally occurring skills, but they can be learned. Personality, of course, plays a part for effective leaders but skill development is also important. An instructor can teach some skills during meetings held with group leaders or in class, but he or she should also provide encouragement and feedback so that students can continue to practice the skills and understand how to improve. This is only one of many reasons why an instructor should know stages of group development, communication skills, conflict resolution skills, and how to intervene to prevent or deal with problem behaviors. It is usually more helpful for an instructor to highlight what leaders are doing correctly and give suggestions for increasing effectiveness rather than to focus on weaknesses or errors.

Observing and Managing

It is very important for instructors to monitor the small group to ensure attention to task, encourage inclusion of all members, and prevent problems and abuses. This task is accomplished through observing how the groups are functioning and managing their structure for the first few meetings, requiring minutes of sessions, and finding a strategy that will allow students to report on progress periodically throughout the course.

When observing, an instructor should resist being drawn into the discussion unless it is absolutely necessary. If questions arise in the group that are addressed to the instructor, answers should be minimal or deferred, as the answers may be useful information for the entire class. That is, the question that emerges in one group is likely to be of concern in another group, and thus should be addressed when the class meets as a whole. Simply determine if the group is correctly focused and provide feedback to the group and leader on observed behavior. Table 3.4 can be used as a guide to provide feedback.

Consulting Role

The instructor's most critical role after groups begin to work is that of consultant. This is also a difficult role, as a consultant typically interacts with a client very differently than does an instructor with students. Both may teach, but they have different approaches to teaching. Further complicating matters is, that although the instructor may function as a consultant, he or she also has an inescapable evaluation role to play; whereas the client is free to reject a consultant's recommendation, students either do not have this option or do not perceive that they have the option. Consultants do not give grades or evaluate,

Table 3.4 Group and Leader Feedback Form

Rating Scale

5	excellent progress	2	fair progress; needs help
4	good progress	1	poor progress
3	adequate progress	0	not applicable

Group

A.	Minutes—overall quality	5	4	3	2	1	0
	Adequacy of information	5	4	3	2	1	0
	Timely submission	5	4	3	2	1	0
	Grammar, punctuation, spelling	5	4	3	2	1	0
B.	Commitment of members—overall level	5	4	3	2	1	0
	Attendance	5	4	3	2	1	0
	Assumption of responsibility	5	4	3	2	1	0
C.	Meetings—overall quality	5	4	3	2	1	0
	Held at instructor-approved sites	5	4	3	2	1	0
	Held at instructor-approved times	5	4	3	2	1	0
	Instructor can observe	5	4	3	2	1	0
	Scheduled when all members can attend	5	4	3	2	1	0
D.	Project—overall quality	5	4	3	2	1	0
	All members involved in planning	5	4	3	2	1	0
	Task assignments	5	4	3	2	1	0
	Completion of tasks	5	4	3	2	1	0
	Progress toward completion	5	4	3	2	1	0
	Meeting the timeline	5	4	3	2	1	0
E.	Leader—Overall rating	5	4	3	2	1	0
	Appropriately structures sessions	5	4	3	2	1	0
	Regularly meets with instructor	5	4	3	2	1	0
	Tries to involve all group members	5	4	3	2	1	0
	Keeps instructor fully informed	5	4	3	2	1	0

but instructors do both; students as well as instructors may have difficulty in separating these roles.

The consultant's role also requires a different approach to communicating with the group. While the instructor-consultant is the "expert," students are the clients. Clients in the "real world" are not likely to react positively to suggestions that they are ignorant, incompetent, stupid, or insensitive. Consultants therefore have to find ways of presenting suggestions that are likely to be positively received and adopted. Thus, instructors also need to keep in mind that they must develop and also model effective communication styles, particularly when they are consultants.

Consulting and Communicating
Instructors-turned-consultants can employ varying techniques to communicate with student/clients to elicit desired responses. I have termed one set of communication techniques "Judgmental and Caring," to reflect some of the characteristic behaviors and attitudes. In this role an instructor is judgmental when:

- Being critical
- Assigning blame
- Expressing opinions
- Declaring what students "should and ought" to be or do

An instructor makes a shift to a caring attitude when:

- Soothing
- Protecting
- Sympathizing
- Empathizing
- Encouraging
- Transmitting values
- Modeling a sense of duty
- Nurturing

All of these behaviors and attitudes, both judgmental and caring, have positive and negative aspects, and all are helpful to the instructional process when used moderately and appropriately. The caring characteristics are especially helpful in the beginning stages of groups when students are confused, anxious, and desirous of structure. Judgmental characteristics used in moderation help set standards and give students guidance for what is acceptable and unacceptable.

I have termed another set of instructor-consultant behaviors and attitudes "Mature and Task-Oriented." In this role, an instructor:

- Analyzes
- Thinks rationally
- Remains objective
- Focuses on facts
- Stays organized
- Evaluates data
- Is responsible
- Solves problems
- Is assertive
- Is direct in interactions

These behaviors and attitudes can be of immense help in solving problems, resolving conflicts, keeping students on track, and modeling desired behaviors and attitudes. They are also very helpful in dealing with students' immaturity and encouraging them to use their creativity.

Generally, students have their own set of behaviors and attitudes, which can be termed "Immature." The immaturity may be transitory, stemming from the ambiguity and tension always present at the beginning of groups, or it may indeed be an ingrained personality trait. An immature person may be:

- Impulsive
- Uncensored
- Self-indulgent
- Self-centered
- Rebellious
- Aggressive
- Withdrawn
- Procrastinating
- Whining
- Demanding

On the other hand, immaturity can also be characterized by spontaneity, intuitiveness, and creativity, which are behaviors and attitudes to be cultivated. Instructors can also be tempted to give immature responses.

Table 3.5 presents some common student remarks that are characteristic of immaturity followed by possible instructor responses characteristic of the Judgmental, Caring, Immature, and Mature categories. Judgmental responses are usually designed to promote guilt and shame. The receiver is made aware of shortcomings, flaws, and disappointing behavior that indicate some failure to live up to expectations. An instructor who uses this communication may be correct in terms of evaluation, but he or she is not building positive relationships, which is especially important for the beginning stages of the class and group work.

Table 3.5 Examples of Instructor Communication Styles

Student asks for information that has already been provided.
Instructor

Judgmental response: "Why don't you read your syllabus?"

Caring response: "Let's go over what's in the syllabus."

Immature response: "I don't know why you can't be responsible enough to read your syllabus."

Mature and task-oriented response: "That information should be in your materials. If it isn't, please let me know because others may also need it."

Student to the instructor: "Will you be doing anything important in class today?"
Instructor

Judgmental response: "You're supposed to attend class."

Caring response: "You're trying to decide if you can miss this class and get the notes from someone."

Immature response: "Of course not. I never do anything important."

Mature and task-oriented response: "I intend to lecture on the project."

Student to the instructor: "Do I need to know this for a test?"
Instructor

Judgmental response: "You ought to want to know this information whether or not it appears on a test."

Caring response: "You're tired of taking notes."

Immature response: "It's up to you if you want to chance it."

Mature response: "I cannot say for sure that this specific information will be the next test but it will be needed at some point for your classwork."

Student to the instructor: "Why do we have to work in groups?"
Instructor

Judgmental response: "You should want to learn how to work cooperatively with others."

Caring response: "You have some apprehension about how well a group will perform."

Immature response: "It is a class requirement."

Mature response: "You have worked independently most of the time and feel that you work best that way. However, the work world generally requires working in teams and this class can help you learn to be effective both ways."

Table 3.5 (*Continued*)

Student to the instructor: "I don't like group work!"
Instructor

Judgmental response: "You are not determining the requirements for this class.
   I am."

Caring response: "You really do not want to participate in a group."

Immature response: "Too bad."

Mature response: "Yours is a usual response for those who have either not worked
   in a group or who have an unpleasant experience in a group. The groups in this
   class will be somewhat different and I hope you will give them a fair chance."

A caring response shows some concern for the receiver. The other person's feelings are heard and understood; this response helps to build relationships. But caring responses are usually not task-oriented and do little to help accomplish the task. Caring responses are generally helpful in the beginning stages of the class and group work to reduce anxiety and promote feelings of confidence and safety.

Immaturity is not limited to students. Instructors can also give immature responses that show a lack of concern for the other person; they can also be demanding, self-centered, or aggressive. Instructors' immature responses are generally a result of frustration. They can be characterized as immaturity meeting immaturity. When an instructor responds this way, he or she neither builds relationships nor aids in accomplishing the task. Neither the instructor nor the student feels positive after an immature exchange.

A mature, responsible comment takes into account not only the speaker's and receiver's needs, but also the requirements of the tasks; that is, both relationship and course needs. The receiver generally does not feel that his or her real message has been ignored, which enhances the relationship. The task is not ignored, either, which helps in attaining it. When instructors use mature responses, students can observe and learn from their modeling of effective communication.

Consulting and Information Giving

The style of communication is only one aspect of the consultant's role. A sense of what and how much assistance is needed is also important. After all, the intent is for students to learn and gain more confidence in their ability to work cooperatively in groups. If an instructor provides too much assistance, students are then working as they would in a regular class, and the value of group work is lost. On the other hand, if an instructor does not provide enough assistance, the group flounders and confidence is eroded.

How much is enough? This is difficult to gauge even when one directly observes a group; it is just about impossible for this book to be definitive. Each group differs in its need for assistance, and all groups differ in their needs from session to session. Given this condition, how can an instructor decide when to give assistance, how much assistance to give, and what assistance would be helpful? An instructor's experience and maturity are of immense benefit in gauging when assistance is enough or when it is smothering or micro-managing. Some basic guidance questions are:

- Are students lacking needed information or skills?
- Have students underused available information and/or members' expertise?
- Are other groups facing the same problems?
- How much time is being spent on the problem?
- Has the task been broken down into sequential steps so that all fully understand what needs to be done and when?
- Are group members very frustrated and do they appear to be floundering?

Some anxiety and frustration are expected any time something new is attempted. There may also be necessary skills or resources lacking. An instructor should not aim to eliminate or prevent anxiety and frustration, as some measure of these states appears to work positively by producing enough tension to push the work forward. However, too much anxiety and frustration retards task accomplishment and learning; an instructor should intervene to assist at this point.

Consulting and the First Group Sessions

An instructor uses both the teaching and the consulting roles when working with student leaders during the first few group sessions. After these sessions are complete, the consultant's role is most important for group meetings and the teaching role is most needed in the classroom for sessions with the entire class.

The first group sessions are crucial for making sure groups understand the task, are headed in the right direction, and have confidence in their abilities. These sessions are also important for group leaders, for this is when group leaders have to deal with not only their personal anxieties but also those of the group members. They also have the task of helping structure the work, making sure all members are included, and dealing with a new, ambiguous situation. For these and other reasons, it is crucial that an instructor meet regularly with group leaders. My practice is to hold a weekly meeting throughout the semester and to be available via the telephone and a half-hour before class for consultation.

Although the instructor has done considerable planning for groups prior to the class, some planning still needs to be done with the group leaders. They usually do not have either education or experience in leading groups and need instruction and guidance. The following list presents the primary strategies an instructor can use.

Be Specific
Since group leaders tend to be novices at leading groups, it is very helpful to provide them with some specifics for conducting the sessions. Asking for a report on what was done in each meeting allows monitoring and makes sure groups are remaining on task and productive. It can be helpful for the instructor to give student leaders specific goals for the first few sessions, such as developing a timeline for task accomplishment, assigning roles and tasks, setting meeting times and dates, and identifying needed resources. The subject matter can dictate what other specifics are needed during the first few sessions.

Provide Just Enough Structure
Asking for more and more structure is one way group members exhibit anxiety in the beginning stages of group. They will ask many questions, say they do not understand, and, even when given more information, continue to protest that they are confused about what to do. Instructors who do not recognize that they are dealing with anxiety rather than a lack of information will try to provide more and more structure yet experience little or no lessening of student questioning. No one can provide sufficient structure to prevent this anxiety; an instructor should resist trying to answer every question and make sure no one is confused.

This is not to say that an instructor should not answer questions; some clarification may always be needed and should be provided. But if the instructor finds that the more information given, the more additional questions arise, most likely student anxiety rather than a lack of information is the problem. Instructors are advised to provide just enough structure so that the task and requirements are sufficiently explained.

Build on Previous Sessions
It is helpful to decide what needs to be done in the next sessions by building on the current and previous sessions. Therefore, it is important for the instructor first to have student group leaders give a brief summary of what transpired, to ask questions about problems and concerns, and to have read the minutes prior to meeting with group leaders.

The instructor needs to be familiar with stages of group and expected behaviors to know better how to build on previous sessions. A fuller discussion of group stages is presented in Chapter 5. Also presented there are some problem behaviors, possible causes or underlying reasons, and suggested strategies for preventing or resolving them. This information can provide student leaders with strategies to further group development and resolve problems.

Solicit Suggestions

One way an instructor can help build group leaders' confidence and also reduce the tendency or likelihood of giving too much assistance is to solicit suggestions from them on how to proceed or solve problems in the group. Further, by asking for suggestions in group meetings with student leaders, there are opportunities for them to help and learn from each other.

At first, group leaders will expect the instructor to be the expert and give them answers. Their attitude may be one of "tell me what to do." It can be tempting to the instructor to try and do so. However, no two groups are alike, and even the most observant and knowledgeable instructor is somewhat removed from the group and lacks essential information about members. Group leaders' suggestions can be surprisingly helpful.

If no useful suggestions emerge or the suggestions are destructive, however, an instructor can propose different ones to consider. At times, an instructor has to directly and firmly say that a student's suggestion is not viable, and give a rationale for not using it. The instructor should avoid, however, characterizing a student's idea as a bad one. Instead, he or she should use a part of it, if possible, to move to a more useful course of action. There are two main purposes for not totally rejecting a student's suggestion: to promote confidence and to help group leaders learn how to develop useful group strategies and interventions.

Block

Holding group meetings for leaders allows an instructor to suitably intervene to block existing or potential problem behaviors. For example, if a group member has not completed the first task assigned, the instructor can investigate and take steps if needed to reduce the impact of this on the group's project. Another example might be a member who is dropping suggestive comments; if not addressed, such behavior could escalate to sexual harassment.

Group leaders are unlikely to have much experience at preventing or addressing problem behaviors such as monopolizing, anger expression, or socializing; it can be especially difficult to do so in a way that promotes group development and does not alienate the offending member. Some common problem behaviors and suggested intervention, blocking, and prevention strategies are discussed in Chapter 7.

Offer Positive Comments

Even group leaders who appear confident appreciate positive comments from the instructor, especially in the beginning stages. They benefit from reassurance that they are meeting the instructor's expectations and that the group is not failing.

"Positive comments" and "praise" are similar but not the same. The second edition of Webster's Unabridged Dictionary (1983) uses words such as *commend, applaud, admire, extol, glorify,* and *magnify* in its definition for *praise.* Too much praise can be misinterpreted as flattery, which is "excessive, untrue, or insincere praise" (Webster's, 1983) and is not likely to build trust.

Positive comments, on the other hand, highlight what is going well or as expected in the group whether or not it is due to the leader's actions. For example, if the leader reports that in the second session all members attended on time and seemed to be interested and involved, a positive comment would focus on how members with those attitudes can get a lot accomplished while praise would ascribe the accomplishment to the impact and influence of the leader.

It is most helpful to group leaders in the beginning stages of group work to emphasize what is being done correctly or to expectation rather than what is weak or needs to be done better. Some problems or conditions work themselves out and others are better addressed after confidence is built and safety established.

Model Group Leadership Skills
An instructor has a unique opportunity to model effective group leadership skills during meetings with group leaders. That too, is a group and the meetings are sessions. These meetings tend to be more task-oriented but they also have a maintenance aspect and move through stages. Chapter 10 presents leadership skills in more detail.

Read Minutes
Read minutes of sessions very carefully, as they tell what is taking place in the various groups, what is not being done that should be done, and clues about potential problems. At meetings with group leaders, ask for clarification of points in the minutes and use common issues as a springboard for agendas for future meetings. Common problems among groups, common misunderstandings, and other points derived from reading minutes can form the instructor's agenda for the group leaders' meetings.

Observe Groups
Another way for instructors to gather information to help groups and leaders is by observing group sessions. The instructor should not necessarily participate, although that can be useful sometimes, but just observe in order to provide constructive feedback and make sure groups are focused well.

When observation is used in this way it gives students a sense of safety, that the instructor is paying attention to the groups. It is also reassuring that even though a group may make a mistake, it will be quickly caught and students will not waste time and effort.

Table 3.6 presents a form that instructors can use to give specific feedback to groups on levels of participation, inclusion of members, observed

Table 3.6 Group Observation Feedback Form

Rating Scale

5	always, or almost always		2	sometimes, infrequently
4	very frequently		1	never, or almost never
3	often		0	unable to observe

	5	4	3	2	1	0
Participation—Overall	**5**	**4**	**3**	**2**	**1**	**0**
Members volunteer input	5	4	3	2	1	0
Members volunteer for tasks	5	4	3	2	1	0
Members do not have to be coaxed to participate	5	4	3	2	1	0
Inclusion of Members—Overall	**5**	**4**	**3**	**2**	**1**	**0**
Members and leader ask for each other's input	5	4	3	2	1	0
Communication Patterns—Overall	**5**	**4**	**3**	**2**	**1**	**0**
Speak directly to each other	5	4	3	2	1	0
Focused on task	5	4	3	2	1	0
Respond directly to input	5	4	3	2	1	0
Nonverbal Behaviors—Overall	**5**	**4**	**3**	**2**	**1**	**0**
Show interest (forward lean, eye contact, open body position)	5	4	3	2	1	0
Positive facial expression	5	4	3	2	1	0
Neutral facial expression	5	4	3	2	1	0

nonverbal behaviors indicating extent of interest shown, and communication skills. These are very basic conditions that characterize differences between productive and unproductive groups. Each topic has associated observable behaviors that are rated by the instructor.

The Instructor's Role in Later Stages

After the beginning stages of groups are completed, groups need less monitoring and observation. Safety and trust are established, to varying extents, which allows group members to focus more on the task and to perceive the instructor increasingly as a consultant. Members will more often seek out the instructor only when help or information is needed. However, there are several instructor tasks that should be continued: weekly or biweekly meetings with group leaders, review of minutes submitted, monitoring, giving groups and leaders feedback, and teaching conflict mediation or conflict resolution skills. An instructor should also be available to attend a group session to act as a mediator when requested or needed.

CHAPTER 4

Developing Student Expertise

One of the most important things a student can learn is how to be an effective group member. This experience is preparation for the world of work, where many tasks are conducted in groups or teams. The ability to work cooperatively or collaboratively is prized by supervisors and bosses, and meta-analyses, such as those by Johnson and Johnson (1992) and Freeberg and Rock (1987), demonstrate the effectiveness and productivity of group over individual outcomes.

Being an effective group member incorporates commitment, communication, conflict resolution, and attention to what to do and what not to do as group members. Some of these can be learned behaviors and attitudes, others rely more on basic personality characteristics, and some are related to the effectiveness of the group leader and the structuring of the group. Even those who feel they work best independently can learn to use these behaviors and attitudes to also work well in groups.

COMMITMENT

Commitment to the group means that members believe in the efficacy of group work and make every effort to ensure the group functions effectively, that all members are respected, and that the work of the group is expedited. These attitudes contribute positively to the functioning of any group—academic or professional

In order for any group to function effectively, members must be willing to contribute their time. This means attending group sessions and being on time. Members who routinely miss meetings, arrive late, and make no effort to notify other group members when they cannot attend meetings are demonstrating their lack of commitment to the group, disregard for what the group and members have to offer, and resistance to the idea of working in groups.

It is also understandable that there are circumstances, such as illnesses and accidents, that contribute to being absent or tardy. However, these are usually few and the responsible group member informs the leader and/or other group members in advance when unable to attend a meeting. Further, the responsible group member wants to make contributions and to help make sure the work is done, and so makes every effort to attend.

Even if one is somewhat skeptical about the efficacy of group work, perhaps because of past experiences or a preference for independent work, one can still make a commitment to do one's best, to attend meetings, and to be on time. In the world of work, many are evaluated on the extent to which they exhibit commitment in their behavior and attitude.

Taking responsibility and being accountable is a vital part of commitment. Responsible behavior demonstrates maturity, dedication, diligence, and persistence, all qualities that contribute to success in any field and, more importantly, facilitate accomplishing the work of the group. Responsibility, in an effective group, is shared by the leader and members. The leader oversees structuring and directing the group, but all members must contribute to the functioning of the group. Behaviors and attitudes reflective of members who assume responsibility are:

- Giving and receiving input
- Willingness to participate in consensual decision making
- Encouraging and modeling effective communication and relationship skills
- Prompt completion of assignments and tasks

The responsible member is also willing to be held accountable for his or her actions—or inaction.

Another indication of commitment is the willingness to work on group matters, both internal and content-based. Internal matters pertain to the functioning of the group, including relationships with other members and the leader, avoidance of participating in a clique, and being an active participant. Content-based group matters refer to the task project and subject material on which the group is working.

Support for other group members is also a part of commitment. Support can be given in many ways. For example, it is supportive to make sure the group allows careful consideration of an unusual opinion rather than disparaging or ignoring it. Members do not have to agree to be supportive, but just be willing to hear everyone out and take what they have to say seriously. Support is also evident when group members work with each other to help learn new or unfamiliar material. Working with each other to help debug a program or understand a principle are examples of supportive behavior.

COMMUNICATION

Chapters 10 through 12 provide an extensive discussion of verbal and nonverbal communication. Presented here is a summary of constructive communication behaviors that contribute positively to the functioning of the group. While few, they are basic and very important.

The first and most important behavior is to give verbal input. Silence contributes to misinterpretation and ambiguous situations. Group members really help the leader and the group when they are verbally responsive. It is much more helpful to say, "I would like to take some time to think about it before I form an opinion," or, "I disagree," or, "I do not have enough information," or, "I feel like we are moving too fast," than it is just to say nothing.

It is also helpful when members volunteer their ideas, opinions, and thoughts, rather than having to be asked directly. The leader cannot know if a person wants to contribute or would rather be left alone to think; if members regularly participate of their own accord, the leader is relieved of this burden. Furthermore, if the leader always has to call on members directly, it makes the group seem more like a class and the leader appear more like an authority figure.

Good communication also involves members talking directly with each other rather than to and through the leader. The tendency is for all communication to be directed at the leader in the beginning stages of group work. Experienced group leaders will recognize what is happening, however, and gently and consistently encourage members to interact and talk directly with each other.

Another important communication behavior is to incorporate ideas from others. When working in a team or group, members seek to feel included. One way of doing this is to try and incorporate their input into discussion and decision making rather than ignore or disparage it. Even if, ultimately, the group decides to drop that part, members feel included if there is effort to use what they contribute.

It will take some awareness and effort, but effective group members try to reduce their personal barriers to communication, such as stereotyping others, wanting to be the center of attention, seeking admiration from others, needing to be considered unique and special, and being impatient with particular thinking and speaking patterns. These behaviors are constraints in understanding others and establishing satisfying relationships with them.

CONFLICT RESOLUTION

Controversy and conflict are expected to be a part of all groups and teams. It is impossible never to have conflict. What often happens, however, is that conflict is suppressed, ignored, or denied. When there are no good-faith efforts to resolve the conflict, the progress of the group is stymied. Ironically, often more time and effort are expended in suppressing, ignoring, and denying than would be used to constructively resolve the conflict. This occurs because many people are afraid of the consequences of conflict, fear the intense feelings generated in themselves and in others during conflict, and do not know how to act in conflict situations, and are unsure how best to proceed.

Specific conflict resolution strategies are presented in Chapter 6. Here, we will simply emphasize the importance of an attitude conducive to recognizing conflicts when they emerge, willingness to allow them to emerge, adoption of a perspective that conflicts can usually be resolved so that neither party "loses," and understanding that all parties have roles to play in conflicts. Just knowing how suppressing conflict can retard the progress of the group, not to mention the negative impact on the quantity and quality of the work produced, should be sufficient to convince members to allow conflicts to emerge and be resolved.

This does not mean that most of the group's time needs to be spent on resolving conflicts. Indeed, when members are able to accept responsibility for their actions and feelings, respect other group members and their rights to differing opinions, use active listening and responding skills, and commit to establishing "win-win" situations, fewer conflicts should arise and those that do are more easily resolved. It is a rare situation that produces enduring conflicts; perhaps one or more members are emotionally disturbed or have poor impulse control. In such instances, the only solution is to remove the member(s) from the group.

WHAT TO DO

Have a Focus

Group members who have personal goals and objectives related to the group are more effective than members who do not. Personal goals and objectives provide structure, focus, and aim, and, when the group is ended, can be used as a yardstick for satisfaction with personal accomplishments. To determine personal goals and objectives, one may wish to ask the following: Given the goal and objectives for the course, what are my personal goals and objectives as far as learning is concerned? What seems most important to me? What can I learn from my group experience? What am I willing to contribute? The very act of asking these questions sharpens one's focus.

Be Flexible

Having a focus does not mean being closed to new ways of behaving, performing, or relating. Effective group members retain enough flexibility to incorporate the new while retaining the positive aspects of the old.

Flexibility means a willingness to consider alternatives, to attempt different approaches, and to adjust to needed changes in thoughts and actions. Flexible group members do not relinquish their deeply held values and convictions, but they are open to exploring other options and alternatives. They do not mindlessly insist on doing things as they have always been done, or only in the way with which they are familiar, nor do they reject out of hand proposals from other members. They take action only after careful consideration.

Be Present-Centered

An effective group member is present-centered; he or she attends each session ready to be in the group and work on the group's task. This may seem to be elementary, but too many group members do not come prepared to work.

For example, some attend sessions in body only; their minds are elsewhere. They are not present-centered, but are emotionally and cognitively elsewhere, so that they are not bringing all of their resources to work on the group's task. Students should try to clear their minds of other concerns when in the group, and give all of their attention to the task at hand.

Express Wants and Needs

Effective group members are very clear in expressing their wants and needs. They may not always be satisfied, but others are not left in doubt as to what they want or need. This openness is very helpful to the group process, as important feelings are not suppressed or ignored.

Wants and needs incorporate many things. Some members want their input taken seriously, others want an opportunity to have input, and still others may want time to reflect before having to come to a decision. For others, conditions may change during the semester so that the agreed-on meeting time is no longer possible. Instead of suffering in silence or ceasing to attend, they should request to have the time changed.

The importance of this openness is also reflected in conflict situations. It is very helpful when a member expresses that he or she wants to work on and resolve a conflict with another member. By saying this directly and openly, everyone else understands that this person is willing to engage in conflict resolution and is concerned about the impact of the conflict on the group. If this person never speaks up, on the other hand, then no one knows that he or she is willing to work on the conflict, the other person involved may feel reluctant to work on it, and the whole situation will take longer to be worked out, if it ever is.

Attend to Feelings

Feelings are the most important part of any communication and effective members are sensitive both to their personal feelings and to the feelings of others. How one feels about something is much more important than what one says about it; if the two are not congruent, others will receive mixed messages.

One does not always have to openly express all feelings, but should just be aware of what they are and to what they are related. For example, it is not necessary to announce, "I am bored," as saying so may not help anyone. However, awareness of one's own boredom, and asking what its cause is, and why one feels turned off, inattentive, annoyed, or angry is much more useful than expressing the feeling. By exploring what may be triggering these feelings, one comes to a better understanding of personal reactions and possible solutions. For example, if a member realizes that her boredom is connected to suppressing annoyance with how a member is storytelling, then she can say something to help refocus the session on the task at hand.

It is also important to give attention to others' feelings, such as frustration, confusion, anger, or feeling overwhelmed. Group members may not always openly express these feelings, but they affect the functioning of the group and, if left unattended, may impair the effectiveness of the members. This does not mean that group members are responsible for making sure that other members do not experience these feelings, or for rushing to make sure that they feel better. Group members are all responsible for their personal feelings. But when you are attentive enough to be aware of others' feelings, then in some instances, you can encourage open expression of them, which may lead to improvement of the situation.

Participate Actively

Effective group members are active participants. "Active" means attending sessions, being on time, working on the group's task, being willing to speak, and participating in decision making and conflict resolution. These are all attitudes and behaviors that help the group and its members to accomplish the goals and objectives.

Experiment with New Ways of Behaving

The group gives members an opportunity to experiment with new ways of behaving. For example, if a member tends to be silent or tentative about speaking, he or she can experiment with becoming more assertive. Such a person might feel ignored. This person could experiment with saying directly to the group that he or she feels ignored, giving other members an opportunity to be more responsive.

Learning which behaviors are valued for team members on the job gives students an opportunity to practice them in classroom groups. For example, what does it mean to be cooperative, both in the work world and in classroom groups? Behaviors that illustrate cooperation are those described in the previous section under active participation. Cooperating does not mean agreeing with everything, doing what someone else wants all or most of the time, or giving up individuality. Mostly, cooperation means being an effective group member.

Remain Open to Receiving and Giving Feedback

Groups are an excellent way to learn more about how others perceive us. We all have a self-perception that has some basis in objective reality, but we all also have blind spots. That is, there are parts of ourselves that are seen by others of which we are not aware. When we are open to feedback in group work, we can expand our awareness of how we come across to others.

This can be very valuable in correcting misperceptions we may have or in making us aware of unrealized strengths. There may even be talents that are underdeveloped because we remain oblivious to their existence. Increasing this awareness by being open to feedback allows us to remediate deficiencies, correct misperceptions, and capitalize on strengths.

Being open to feedback means not automatically being on the defensive, rejecting or ignoring comments about how others perceive us. It means reserving judgment and remaining willing to consider the merits of what is said about us. Sometimes, it means not taking remarks personally, but accepting that another person's opinion might have merit and should be considered.

A willingness to provide constructive feedback is also important. (Constructive feedback is described in more detail in Chapter 8.) Constructive feedback gives an individual helpful information about him- or herself from the sender's perspective. For example, a group member who feels that he or she does not have much to contribute could be helped by feedback from group members on how they perceive his or her contributions. They could express appreciation for how that person keeps the group reminded of the primary focus, or tell how that person's smile, when others enter the room, makes them feel welcomed.

Constructive feedback can also highlight behaviors that detract from the person's effectiveness about which they seem unaware. For example, constructive feedback would be to point out that someone's tendency to make disparaging remarks about himself makes it seem that he does not consider himself competent, but that others do not share this impression.

Maintain Confidentiality

It will be the rare group in which a member, or members, do not disclose personal material that is better kept confidential. This material may be anything from a negative comment about the class, instructor, or someone else to significant personal disclosures. Members feel safer in the group when they can trust group members not to repeat comments to anyone outside the group.

Although the instructor is considered a member of the group and much is reported to him or her, group members need to feel that the group is a safe place to let off steam when needed.

There are situations, however, in which keeping a confidence is counterproductive or even illegal. Violation of university policies, threats of violence, harassment, or other menacing behaviors should be reported to the instructor. Knowledge of violations of laws may result in personal liability if not reported. Threats of suicide should always be taken seriously and reported. Clearly, however, it is only extreme situations that require breaking confidentiality. Similarly, most careers and jobs have requirements and guidelines for what must be reported; those who fail to do so can be held liable or even lose their jobs.

Learn about Nonverbal Behavior

The most accurate and greatest part of the message in interpersonal communication is nonverbal behavior. Words convey content; body position, gestures, and voice tone and inflection convey attitudes and feelings, both spoken and unspoken. These are some of the reasons why it is important to pay attention to both one's own and others' nonverbal communication. Effective communicators make their verbal and nonverbal message congruent.

Careful observation and accurate readings of gestures, body positions, and voice tone and inflection are helpful in ascertaining what someone's real message is. Further, one should become aware of one's own nonverbal behavior and begin to make it congruent with verbal behavior. This is important because what people tend to unconsciously respond to is the real message, as conveyed by nonverbal behavior. This can lead to considerable confusion if what is being said seems to be ignored and something else responded to. For example, a person who is angry but either does not wish to admit it or is not aware of it may deny being angry, even though his or her face and body positions all convey a message of anger. Despite the denial, he or she is likely to be treated as angry. That person, in turn, will begin to wonder why others are being so tentative and may then become hurt or defensive, and withdraw or lash out.

Another example is when a group member's body position screams indifference, but when challenged, he or she asserts that that position is comfortable and not a sign of indifference. The reaction of other group members is to leave that person out or to become hostile because the indifference is perceived as contempt. When workers appear indifferent on the job, it is noted but not always brought to their attention, thereby having a negative impact on others' perceptions and even their evaluations.

Nonverbal behavior is discussed in more detail in Chapter 8.

Take Responsibility

Effective group members do not expect the group leader or the instructor to assume the responsibility for their learning and growth. These people practice the behaviors that characterize active participation. They have goals and objectives for their learning and come to each session prepared to do something to accomplish those goals. They do not sit back and expect or wait for someone to define their learning for them.

For example, if the group work is to produce a document for a project, these group members work to understand the task, secure resources, ask for help when needed, give help to other members, and stay focused on the task of learning. What they do not know or have, they seek out rather than waiting for someone to give it to them.

Responsible group members do not whine and complain that they are not getting what they want or need. They are reluctant to blame others and, even when others have been deficient, are likely to move ahead instead of remaining mired in recriminations.

Help to Resolve Conflicts

The existence of conflicts in every relationship is a given. Some conflicts are minor and easily resolved, while some are serious and can ruin relationships. Every group can expect to have some conflicts and how members choose to deal with these—or not—can have significant implications for the growth, development, and task accomplishment of the group.

It was previously noted that members' willingness to engage in conflict resolution contributes positively to the functioning of the group. This willingness is a characteristic of effective group members. They do not actively seek conflicts, but they do not ignore or seek to suppress conflict either. They understand that conflicts are common, expect that conflicts can be resolved, and believe that relationships in the group can be strengthened by openly and actively dealing with conflicts rather than ignoring or suppressing them.

Conflict and resolution are discussed in Chapters 6 and 8. Chapter 6 presents specific conflict resolution strategies and Chapter 8 describes how conflict is expected, emerging in stage two of group development.

Develop Communication Skills

One of the things that can be learned or further developed in classroom groups is communication skills. Effective group members either have or learn facilitative communication skills, which means that they seek to reduce personal barriers to accurate listening so that they not only hear content from the speaker, they understand the deeper meaning. The effective group member appreciates the value of attending to others, showing interest while listening, and responding directly.

Group members are likely to come in with differing levels of facilitative communication skill, but such skills will be of value in group and work situations. They are presented in Chapters 10 through 12; a brief description of two important points follows below.

Speak Directly to Individual Group Members
This may appear to be a somewhat elementary characteristic of an effective group member, but many group members do not do this, especially in the beginning stages of the group. Almost every person will directly address the leader or the entire group, but will not speak directly to other members individually. Almost no one is called by name, responded to by noting agreement or disagreement with what was said, or asked for their input.

Effective members attend to other group members, call them by name, maintain eye contact when speaking to them, orient their bodies toward the speaker, and directly address other individuals rather than speaking to the group at large all or most of the time. They do not use the leader as a conduit for speaking to other members, nor do they wait for the leader to ask other members for input.

Members feel included and valued when others look at them, use their names, and speak directly to them. Effective group members facilitate the process of becoming cohesive by practicing this behavior.

Respond Directly
Responding directly can be difficult for some people because their usual manner of response does not incorporate paraphrasing, asking for clarification, or summarizing. A direct response first acknowledges what the other person has said by using words that reflect what the hearer thought was said or meant. How often do misunderstandings and misperceptions occur because this step in communicating is omitted? More often than we like to admit.

At other times, people are so eager to get their opinions, ideas, and thoughts out that they give little attention to previous speaker(s). It is almost as if the other persons have not spoken. Most of this behavior is unintentional, but it still has an impact. People do not feel listened to, heard, or understood when they do not receive a direct response after they speak. The group is a good opportunity to practice giving direct responses, so that doing so becomes a part of one's usual communicating pattern and style.

Summary

These "do" behaviors and attitudes suggested for effective group membership are not all-inclusive. However, they are the most basic and will facilitate group development and help produce more satisfaction for members.

On the other hand, some behaviors and attitudes are best avoided when becoming a group member. The first step in modifying, eliminating, or avoiding these behaviors or attitudes is awareness. Many of the "don'ts" are unconscious behaviors and attitudes that must become conscious before change can occur.

THE DON'TS OF GROUP MEMBERSHIP

Waiting

Avoid waiting to work or become involved in the group. Some tentativeness is expected at the beginning of the group, when members are not sure if they will fit in, be included, or trust other members or the leader. These concerns will likely be worked through in time, though, and are not sufficient reasons to delay work and involvement.

Suppressing Feelings

It was previously noted that "sitting on" or suppressing important feelings has a negative impact on the group's development. Therefore, this is one behavior that effective group members avoid. While they need not reveal every felt emotion, they do express the important ones. For example, it could be important for group members to know that someone is very uncomfortable with or offended by jokes being told. Other group members then know what this person values and can adapt their behavior accordingly. Further, when one person openly expresses such feelings, the group may find that there are others, also.

Making Snap Evaluations and Judgments

Effective group members avoid making quick evaluations and judgments about other members. First impressions are important and tend to endure, but it is wiser to test the validity of these first impressions before forming evaluations or judgments.

Our impressions of others are perceived through our experiences, likes, dislikes, and personalities. In short, our immediate impressions are, like ourselves, usually flawed. Knowing this should make us pause and reserve judgment until we have more evidence, particularly more objective evidence.

Accepting and nonjudgmental group members greatly facilitate the development of safety and trust in the group, leading to group cohesiveness that, in turn, enhances group productivity. It is not enough for the leader alone to be accepting and nonjudgmental; group members must also contribute. These characteristics are presented in more depth in Chapter 10.

Expecting Others to Understand

The need, or desire, to have others understand one's particular situation, perspective, problem, and so on may produce behaviors and attitudes that can be detrimental to the group's functioning and members' participation. Some of these behaviors and attitudes are storytelling, withdrawing or being silent, being sullen, and showing contempt. Furthermore, a person who equates understanding with agreement imagines that anyone who disagrees does not understand. Such a person may then waste even more time and effort in trying to get "understanding."

Effective group members are pleased when they seem to be understood by other group members, but do not expect or need to be fully understood. They avoid prolonged explanations of personal concerns, do not keep returning to a subject or point about which they feel others' understanding is incomplete, do not withdraw emotionally from the group when they feel misunderstood, and do not become sullen to punish members for their failure to understand.

Expecting to Understand Others

It is also not realistic to expect to fully understand others. Each person has unique experiences, personality, and perspectives. People tend to understand best those individuals who are most similar, and to feel that these people do understand (Brown, 1996). However, some individuals can spend large amounts of group time unproductively because of their expectation that they should, or need, to understand completely. They continue to question and encourage storytelling to gather more information so that they can feel they "understand."

Effective group members are content to have sufficient information and incomplete understanding. They are comfortable with some ambiguity, which can also be expected in most work situations.

Giving Advice

A common behavior for many group members in the beginning stages of group is to give advice, both solicited and unsolicited. Members rush to solve each others' "problems" and feel that situations can be "fixed."

Providing needed information is not the same as giving advice. For example, referring someone to a particular office that deals with his or her problem or concern is helpful. This information explains where to go if the person chooses. Giving advice, on the other hand, is telling a person what he or she "should" do.

Effective group members learn the difference between giving information and giving advice. Even when directly asked for advice, they resist doing so. Even solicited advice can be risky for, as was noted previously, it is almost impossible to fully understand another person's perception or situation. Even when the circumstances appear to be similar, what was applicable or effective for one person may not be transferable to another. What one can communicate is the perceived similarities in the two situations, one's own actions, and the results or outcomes. Doing it this way conveys information without telling the other person what to do. It may also be helpful to add that one person's experience may not be applicable to another's circumstances.

Ascribing Motives

Interpreting or ascribing motives for a person's behavior, feelings, or attitudes is likely to produce considerable resistance and/or defensiveness in that person. This, in turn, is detrimental to establishing good relationships and to communication; effective group members will avoid doing this.

Interpretation refers to telling others that they are doing or feeling something because of something about them. By ascribing motives the inference is that they should stop whatever they are doing or feeling, or that they are in some way inadequate or flawed. For example, it would be ascribing motives to tell a member that he or she is not supporting or agreeing to an idea because the member is angry with the person who suggested the idea. It is easy to see how this statement would produce resistance and defensiveness. At the very least, it does not seem helpful to communications or relationships in the group.

Group members should restrict their comments about each other to what was done or said, and not make inferences about why it was done or said. When the focus remains on observable behavior, it is more likely to be objective. Another problem with interpretations is they are likely to be wrong. It is difficult to definitively know why someone does or feels what he or she does. One may be correct in an inference, but one may also be wrong; either way, making inferences does not strengthen relationships or facilitate communications.

Questioning Inappropriately

The effective group member restricts questions to requests for needed information. Avoid rhetorical questions, questions designed to elicit desired responses, or questions that produce emotional intensity or distress. None of these types of questions help the group to do its job or facilitate relationship-building.

One reason for reducing or eliminating unnecessary questions is that asking too many questions of someone may make him or her feel attacked. Someone who feels attacked may shut down, go on the offensive, or become defensive. These are all counterproductive behaviors. The questioner may have the intention of trying to better understand, but the impact on the other person is negative.

Another reason to change questioning behavior is that to make direct statements or ask plainly for what one wants or needs is to be open and genuine. These are all positive communication skills that enhance and promote relationships in the group and accomplishment of the group's task.

Questioning is discussed further in Chapter 10.

Gossiping

Gossiping is defined as "trifling, often groundless rumor, usually of a sensational or intimate nature; idle talk" (American Heritage Dictionary, 1976). Many who engage in gossiping are not trying to be malicious. They are interested in what is happening and want to hear what others know or think. Some gossip is malicious, however, and even gossip without evil intent can end up being very harmful to the person under discussion.

The primary reason for eliminating or avoiding gossip is to build feelings of safety and trust in the group. Group members are more likely to be wary of being open and honest in the group when they have reason to fear that what they say and do will be talked about outside the group. This fear is fueled when they observe group members gossiping about others, even those not in the group, because they cannot be assured that they will not be talked about in other settings. In other words, behavior in the group is reflective of behavior outside the group; if someone engages in gossip in the group, there is every reason to believe that that person will do so outside the group.

Participating in a Clique

Cliques are very destructive to a group. Cliques can be thought of as a group within a group. This "inner group" excludes other group members, is more supportive and protective of its own members than of outsiders, produces feelings of mistrust and lack of safety, and heightens the fears of group members not included in the clique.

Cliques form when part of a group bands together for mutual support and excludes others. They form for many reasons, including existing or new relationships, power, and protection. Cliques can also form without members consciously setting out to do so.

Cliques that form because of existing or new friendships are somewhat natural. These are people who are drawn to each other because of similarities, interests in common, previous associations, or other kinds of close relationships. These members either associated outside the group prior to the group's formation, or have banded together since the group began.

Sometimes cliques form to gain power. Members band together because they can better accomplish their own goals, which may be different from those of other members or the group. This banding together can be particularly effective when group decisions are made by majority vote and the clique votes as a unit. Such a clique can be influential in determining how the group will spend its time and effort, especially if the leader is unaware either of the clique or of how to combat its influence on the group.

Cliques can also form to protect. A subset of group members may have a common concern that is threatening to each of its members. For example, because of past negative personal experiences, some group members fear any open expression of anger. They can form a clique to make sure that no open expressions of anger occur in the group. Whenever any member not in the clique expresses any irritation, annoyance, or displeasure, the clique operates to put the person on the defensive so that the anger, regardless of level or intensity, cannot be openly expressed. This situation is very detrimental to the group's development.

Using Sarcasm

Sarcasm is a way of indirectly expressing feelings, playing the game of one-upmanship, and showing others to be deficient. The underlying message is that the other person is stupid, inept, and flawed and that the speaker is none of these. This communication style is, obviously, not conducive to developing constructive relationships. Effective group members avoid sarcastic remarks and try to use more constructive ways of getting their points across. Chapter 9 presents information on constructive and effective communication.

Displaying Hostility Indirectly

Along with avoidance of sarcasm, effective group members also avoid expressing hostility indirectly. They do not avoid feeling hostile or angry, but instead try to be aware of when they feel this way, attempt to understand what triggered these feelings, and express them openly and directly. They accept responsibility for feeling this way and do not project the feelings on others or try to hide their anger through indirect expression.

A common example of indirect expression of hostility in group work is for a member to agree to do something and then "forget" to do it. Others can then be in the position of seeming to overreact if they berate the forgetful one, when what is really happening is that the forgetter did not want to do the task. The person may in fact be unaware of the hostility that he or she cannot accept the failure as deliberate, and insists that it was an understandable mistake.

Another example of indirectly expressing hostility is when someone plays dumb or helpless. It is obvious that they do have the ability needed, but continue to maintain that they do not know how to it, or make other excuses. It would be much more open and direct if they were to say that they did not want to do it.

Either direct or indirect hostility can be detrimental to the group. When expressed directly it arouses members' fears of violence and makes them uncomfortable; they begin to want to ignore or discount the hostile person's input, and/or dread attending meetings. They are very aware that they cannot know what to expect from the other person and this lowers feelings of safety and trust.

When expressed indirectly, hostility stays just below the level of awareness so that it is felt but not addressed. Members are uncomfortable and do not feel safe but are unable to understand or express what is making them feel the way they do. They too may dread attending meetings but do not have an identified source for these feelings.

Labeling

Labeling occurs when a person's multifaceted and complex nature is ignored in favor of one characteristic, usually a negative one, and an evaluation is made based on this characteristic. Labeling tends to focus on perceived differences, flaws, or weaknesses and to ignore unfamiliar qualities or strengths. Effective group members recognize that others are more likely to respond positively to being perceived as whole persons, particularly in terms of their strengths, and so do their best not to perceive others narrowly.

Disparaging Input from Others

Effective group members want to encourage input from others and do not disparage others' ideas, opinions, thoughts, and feelings. People do not feel that their input is wanted or valued when they encounter disparaging remarks.

It is particularly important to accept input from others even when one does not agree with what is said. The most positive approach is to acknowledge the other person's point or position, explain that one's own differs, and then state that point or position. It is very negative to disparage what others feel or say, as it implies that they are wrong. We are each entitled to our opinions; when they are disparaged, we do not feel included in the group.

SUMMARY

Effective and ineffective behaviors and attitudes in a group can be learned. Most students will not have received any instruction in how to be an effective group member, nor will they know what behaviors and attitudes are considered to be ineffective or counterproductive. This chapter covered some specifics that can guide both the instructor and the student in better understanding how to contribute to the positive functioning of the group.

CHAPTER 5

The Group Performance Curve

In ideal situations the student group leader has been trained prior to leading the group in leadership skills, including effective communication, an understanding both of how groups function and of personal leadership style. However, the reality for most classroom groups is that student group leaders lack this training. Those who do, however, can make a considerable impact on the functioning of the group and satisfaction of group members.

This chapter focuses on important tasks for and characteristics of group leaders and how these are associated with expected member behaviors as the group moves through developmental stages. Particular attention is given to the process of selecting, guiding, and evaluating group leaders. The chapter assumes that neither the student group leader nor the instructor has much or any group leadership experience.

BASIC LEADER CHARACTERISTICS AND SKILLS

It is sometimes difficult to separate characteristics from skills needed for effective group leaders. The following distinction is used for this discussion. Characteristics refer to internal states, such as attitudes, that are a part of a person's personality. These are ingrained, although subject to modification through experiences. That is, attitudes can change. Skills, on the other hand, are defined as learned behaviors. For example, a group leader can be taught when and how to block monopolizing to stop the behavior without alienating the member or others in the group.

Effective group leaders have the following characteristics:

- Faith in group process
- Awareness

- Tolerance
- Acceptance

Characteristics

Faith
Faith is belief in the group process: a conviction that group work is a valuable way to accomplish different tasks, that groups can and do function to the benefit of their members, that conflicts can be constructively worked through, and that all group members can make positive contributions. Belief in group process also includes a firm conviction that the group can manage its development with guidance from the leader; that something important is always happening in the group, even when it appears to be at a standstill; and that the group needs a mixture of emphasis on task and relationships. Effective group leaders begin with the faith that their groups can work.

Awareness
Awareness of members' emotional states and communication abilities, as well as awareness of undercurrents in the group, is also characteristic of effective group leaders. Such knowledge allows leaders to capitalize on members' strengths, make constructive use of their abilities, understand when emotional intensity is present or increases, constructively confront, and know when and how to intervene. Awareness provides the group leader with cues for what, how, and when to act, and helps him or her deal with the unexpected.

Tolerance
Tolerance of ambiguity and of diversity is a crucial characteristic of group leaders. The beginning stage of any group can appear very ambiguous to group members, as they search for safety, similarities, inclusion, and trust; dealing with so many unknowns produces considerable anxiety. The group leader manages or contains the anxiety by modeling understanding and acceptance of the ambiguity. Group members feel safer and more trusting when the group leader appears to be comfortable with this ambiguity.

Tolerance of diversity—both intellectual and cultural—is also crucial. Differences between members, opinions, ideas, and values can enrich a group or, if not tolerated, can destroy the group. Lack of tolerance for diversity leads to conflict, scapegoating, exclusion, and alienation. The group leader has to model how to maintain one's own values but also listen to and respect others' values. Intellectual and cultural diversity are very likely to be found in every work setting. Tolerance of such diversity is very crucial learning for students, who may not be fully aware of how much diversity they will encounter in their work.

Acceptance

Acceptance is related to tolerance, as it refers to valuing and respecting each and every group member. In order to be accepting, one also has to be able to tolerate those who are different, whether the difference stems from race, class, culture, ethnic background, or other qualities. A group leader must exhibit behavior and attitudes that demonstrate value and respect for group members. This means that the group leader verbally and nonverbally welcomes members to sessions; makes sure that members' input is solicited or presented; blocks any and all attempts to devalue or disparage members or their ideas; and listens to all members.

Skills

There are many group leadership skills that can be taught and learned. Our focus is on:

- Organizing
- Communicating
- Mediating
- Relationship building

Most student group leaders will have some level of these skills but they will likely be either low or undeveloped. It is the responsibility of the instructor to guide students in developing and refining these skills. Some skills, such as communicating and relationship building, are important for both group leaders and members and can be taught to both—if not directly, then by instructor example. For more information on communication and relationship skills, see Chapter 9.

Organizing

Organizational skills structure the group and its work. Deciding what needs to be done, in what sequence, when tasks should be accomplished, and who has various responsibilities constitute organizing. Much organizing is done by the instructor when planning for classroom groups, but considerable organizing remains to be done within each group. This organizing is a major responsibility for the group leader, who will structure the process so that members understand the group's task. Note, however, that the most effective group leaders involve group members in making decisions.

Another piece of organization concerns the mechanics of the group meetings. Scheduling, securing locations for, and making sure members are aware of meetings are all very important. The minutes also require attention to detail. Even if another group member is taking the minutes, the leader may also need to follow up to ensure the minutes are complete, accurate, and submitted to members and the instructor. Such matters may appear to be minor, but the group leader that attends to them provides some safety and trust for group members that they can and will be successful. Further, group leaders gain experience in organizing group tasks.

Communicating

The importance of communication skills for group work cannot be overestimated. Johnson and Johnson (1997) point out how groups that have a cooperative orientation use styles of communication that differ from groups that have a competitive orientation. Cooperative groups have communications that are open, honest, direct, and accurate.

Competitive groups tend to have communications that are closed, misleading, and indirect, because the goal is to gain an advantage. Needed information may be withheld, distorted, or given to only a few members, leading to lack of trust between members. Competition is viewed by some as a means of making members work up to their potential in hopes of a better reward, but there is considerable empirical evidence that cooperative groups accomplish tasks better, attain more goals, and establish better working relationships. All these are sufficient reasons for promoting skill in communicating.

Mediating

Mediation is what the group leader does to help members resolve conflicts. When disputes are mediated, the group leader demonstrates how to constructively deal with conflicts rather than ignoring them, denying them, or having them harm members and/or the group.

Since conflict exists in every group, leaders need to expect it, recognize it even when it is covert or indirect, and be ready and willing to work through it. This attitude alone will teach group members not to fear conflict, and skillful leaders teach members how to make conflicts constructive experiences.

Mediation is discussed in Chapter 6. Specific guidelines and strategies are presented for the instructor and student group leader as this will be a very important skill for the classroom group and in the workplace.

Relationship-Building

Of equal importance to accomplishing the task in a classroom group is building relationships. Groups need to learn how to balance task and relationship functions, as both are necessary for a fully functioning, cooperative, and productive group. The group leader can do much to model relationship-building skills, which, in turn, teaches group members what they are and how they impact the group.

Relationship-building skills that can be developed include:

- Helping members talk directly to each other
- Clarifying what is heard

- Responding directly to others
- Expressing important feelings in the group
- Openly showing support and encouragement
- Considering other perspectives and incorporating them into decisions
- Working out differences
- Being present-centered

These may sound simple but are in fact very complex and can be difficult to do. Specific strategies and guidelines are presented in Chapter 9.

Summary

Although the previous discussion described basic characteristics and skills of group leaders, for most classroom groups these will be goals rather than starting points. That is, the most instructors can expect is for student leaders to develop these skills as a result of their experiences with the group. Further, they and the instructor will become more aware that developing these characteristics and skills is an ongoing process that continues with each group experience.

GROUP LEADER SELECTION PROCESS

There are four basic methods for determining who will be group leader:

- Appointment
- Volunteering
- Election
- Allowing a natural leader to emerge

Each of the above four methods will be presented, describing the pros and cons. Several other leader selection techniques will also be discussed.

Appointment

The instructor can appoint the group leaders. This may be particularly desirable when an instructor knows students' abilities and leadership potential or has worked previously with students. The most obvious argument against appointment, however, is that the leader is immediately perceived as favored. This means that some members will do everything they can to be perceived favorably by the leader so that, by extension, they too will be favored by the instructor. Other students may not trust or perceive the group leader accurately because he or she was picked.

Other students may become resentful that they were not given the same opportunity. They may become openly defiant or uncooperative, but are more likely to express their displeasure indirectly by promoting dissention in the groups or taking "cheap shots" at the leaders. These behaviors and attitudes can have a serious negative impact on the group.

Volunteering

Another method for determining the group leader is to ask for volunteers. The instructor can describe the tasks, expectations, and rewards for the leader and ask who is willing to assume the role.

A positive aspect of volunteer leaders is that assuming the responsibility is an active choice for the student. The instructor is not forcing or manipulating students; they self-select. Another positive point is that every student has the opportunity to be considered for the position; there are no predetermined favorites.

One downside to asking for volunteers is that the quickest and most aggressive student may rush to volunteer while the quieter, more reflective student is still considering the job. This can result in a better-qualified student not being selected; in some cases, the student who rushes to volunteer may be the least able for the job.

Of course, sometimes no one, or not enough students, will volunteer. Then instructors have the options of waiting until someone is uncomfortable enough to speak up, or selecting someone.

Election

After groups are formed, the instructor can instruct them to elect a leader as their first task. This procedure is perceived as democratic. Some may feel that there is a greater commitment to the leader because he or she was chosen by the members.

What happens all too often in these circumstances, however, is that there is not an election. An election implies that there is some competition, but in many student groups the task becomes instead to find one person who will do the job. The election then becomes a pro forma matter in which whoever agrees to be leader is "elected."

If it turns out that there is in fact more than one person who wants the job and an election is held, the group then has to accommodate a "winner" and a "loser." This is very uncomfortable for everyone: winner, loser, and members who had to make a choice. None of this helps to building positive relationships in the group.

Natural Leader

Allowing the leader to emerge naturally is based on the assumption that some people are born leaders, and given enough time, they either self-select or are selected by the group. Unfortunately, there is seldom enough time available for classroom groups to use this option. Further, if the instructor needs to work with the leader to help direct and facilitate the group, he or she needs to do so from the very beginning of the group; this is not possible if the leader has not yet emerged.

Other Methods of Selecting Group Leaders

There are other methods for determining the group leader, such as sharing leadership among members, rotating leadership among two or three members, or designating oversight roles for every member that eliminate the need for the title or overall responsibility of one group leader. While these methods allow several group members to experience group leadership, they can also be difficult to implement successfully.

When leadership is shared, each member assumes the role for a short period, or there is never a designated group leader but each member is expected to take on whatever role the group needs at a particular time. Effective groups may develop to the point where members can and do share leadership responsibilities, but it takes time and considerable sophistication and comfort on the part of members to get to that point, which is unlikely to be the case for members of classroom groups. They do not have the experience or skill to allow them to be comfortable or function well under this kind of shared leadership.

Rotating leaders allows every member to experience what it feels like to be the leader, even if only for a brief period. This method can produce considerable anxiety, however, because members must constantly adjust to having a new leader, and to changing their roles from members to leader and back again. I use this method to introduce students to the role of leader, but my purpose for groups in my course is to teach group dynamics, not to complete a project. Rotating leaders may not be advisable for other types of classroom groups.

One variation of rotating leaders that may be feasible for some classroom groups is to rotate leadership among two or three members. This could be particularly useful if there is more than one project during the class, and so there could be a different leader for each project. In this way, more than one person gets to experience what it means to be a group leader, and the shifts in leadership are directly and logically tied to shifts in the content-based tasks.

The final method—to determine in advance what roles need to be filled in the group and assign each member to a role—can be beneficial to group members but is complex for the instructor. In effect, there is no group leader. This method poses the risk that someone will not fulfill a role, that the group will lose its focus and direction, or that a role whose importance was not anticipated will not be created. An instructor must have a deep understanding of critical roles for a particular group to use this method. It is not sufficient simply to assign task accomplishment roles, such as scheduling or meetings; one must also assign group maintenance roles, and these are more difficult to conceptualize.

Additional problems that may arise with the no-leader method are that students may forget or be ignorant of the demands of their assigned roles, and so do not perform the necessary tasks. While this is also true for any single leader, it is much easier for the instructor to work with one person on responsibility and needed skills. This method will likely prove very complex and frustrating for both the instructor and the students, especially if the focus is on a body of content and not on the group process, for the time necessary for the group's concerns will erode time available for content.

INSTRUCTOR PREPARATION FOR THE GROUP LEADER

The instructor will have the primary responsibility for preparing the group leader. The instructor should provide the leader with a list of basic task-related events and expectations More difficult to provide the group leader are guidelines and instruction for leading or facilitating the group. The difficulty arises from the complexity and ambiguity that characterize groups and from instructors' own lack of knowledge about group dynamics and group leadership. It is difficult enough for someone knowledgeable in the field to convey this information, and presents a formidable task for someone who has little or no knowledge about group leadership and group dynamics.

However, the intent of this book is to provide both an instructor and a group leader with basic information and strategies to develop group leadership skills. The book can be used as a resource as group work progresses, since it is impossible to teach group leaders everything they need to know before or even after the group begins; trying to give them too much information is overwhelming and counterproductive. Measured and moderate learning will result in more retention.

Task Preparation Guidelines

The instructor should give the group leader specific expectations for scheduling group meetings, meeting with the instructor, providing minutes of meetings, attendance, and reporting problems and problem behaviors. Because this information is also on the syllabus, it is known to both members and leaders. However, the guidelines for group leaders should probably be a separate handout, more detailed than the syllabus's description, to help give novice group leaders more confidence and support.

An example of information to be spelled out in more detail for leaders consists of suggestions for how to structure the assignment, that is, the project. For example, if the project can be separated into individual tasks, the leader can make a list of the tasks prior to the group meeting and ask members to volunteer, or the leader can invite the group to develop its own task list according to members' interests and abilities. Giving alternative ways of structuring the task is helpful to group leaders.

Another task that could be presented would be how to develop a timeline for completion of tasks. The timeline could be developed in conjunction with group members, with each task specified, the person responsible, and the date needed for completion. Allowing students to develop the timeline:

- Gives them experience with the activity
- Helps to promote commitment and a sense of responsibility
- Provides a visual demonstration of what is needed to accomplish the task

The timeline can also be used as a monitoring device.

The group leader can also be particularly helpful in giving the group its direction, defining member roles, securing needed resources and information, and keeping the group on task. The instructor's guidelines should provide specific strategies to accomplish these tasks, as well.

Direction

Direction for the group refers to clear goals, objectives, strategies to accomplish the goals, and an understanding of how members can evaluate progress. The group leader, with the group, should review the instructor's goals and either refine them or redefine them. The goals were developed for the class, not for the specific group, and it is not unusual for some minor or major tweaking to be needed for the goals to better fit the needs of the group. For example, an instructor may have a goal of developing critical thinking skills. The group could decide to redefine that goal to be more specific—developing skills in critiquing research articles—so that they have a better understanding of the task. If the instructor considers this new goal a mechanism for developing critical thinking skills, then it will be an acceptable alternative for the particular group. The point of reviewing the goals is to build commitment for group members. This is not wasted time but a necessary step.

Securing Resources and Information

The group leader does not have sole responsibility for securing needed information and resources, but is responsible for directing the process at the group level. The instructor can facilitate this task by providing information in the guidelines for the group leader, particularly potential sources of information, such as contact persons in the community, literature citations, or offices on campus. For example, if the project were to develop and present seminars or workshops on career education, the instructor could prepare a resource list of community agencies complete with names of directors and telephone numbers.

Identifying sources for needed information can also be done by the group leader and group. It is much more efficient for the group to decide what resources are needed and designate one person to identify where they are located than to have several people trying to find the same thing. Students have more confidence in the group leader, the instructor, and their own competence when useful information is provided or, at least, its need anticipated. They can develop more faith that the group will be productive and that they will not flounder.

Keeping the Group Focused
Keeping the group on task is another job for the group leader, and the instructor can provide some suggestions in the guidelines for how to do so. The group leaders should know that, while this is an important responsibility, it is not theirs alone; the instructor will assist. Scheduled meetings with the instructor are designed to help leaders devise ways to help the group stay on task. Conversely, minutes and regular meetings give an instructor several ways of determining if students are going in the right direction or if they do not have a good understanding of what they are to do. When the instructor works with the group leader to clarify what actions are needed, the leader's role is enhanced, and members are helped when the leader then clarifies things to them.

Group Facilitation Guidelines

In addition to keeping on top of task-related responsibilities, group leaders must facilitate the group process in every meeting. As noted earlier, they will need help from instructors to do so. Fundamental group facilitation considerations for the student leader are:

- Preparation
- Attitudes
- Inclusion
- Communicating
- Decision making
- Conflict resolution
- Summarizing

Communicating is presented in Chapter 9; and conflict resolution is presented in Chapter 6. This discussion will highlight guidelines for preparation, attitudes, inclusion, and summarizing.

Preparation
Preparation refers to organizing the work, related responsibilities, and environmental (physical space and equipment) concerns, including arranging the room, preparing any handouts, having copies of instructions, and planning for

any special equipment, if needed. Attention to these tasks provides an atmosphere of caring and safety that fosters development of trust. When student leaders carefully prepare for the group they see the positive outcomes that occur, which encourages them to continue this task. Group members also learn how important it is through experiencing positive outcomes.

Attitudes

Appropriate attitudes for a group leader include faith in the efficacy of group work, tolerance and respect for diversity among members, acceptance of each group member as worthwhile and unique, lack of defensiveness, and ability to tolerate ambiguity. These are basic attitudes that are conveyed to members by the leader's behavior. They facilitate group development and do much to promote positive feelings about working in groups.

Inclusion

Inclusion is an important concept for group. If the group is to be effective and productive each member must make a contribution. While it is possible to get the project accomplished when not all members contribute, such a situation is a failure of the group. One of the major reasons for instituting classroom groups is to teach how to accomplish a task using all the resources of the group, that is, its members. Studies continue to show the superiority of group productivity over individual for may tasks (Johnson & Johnson, 1992; Frieberg & Rock, 1987). So it is important for the instructor to guide the group leader in how to make members feel included so that they have a commitment to the group and its task.

Summarizing

Summarizing is one task or responsibility that falls primarily on group leaders. They should be encouraged to end each group session with a summary of what transpired during the meeting as well as to practice giving summaries during the session to recap where the group is. These interim summaries can help keep the group on track and provide benchmarks for the group. Sometimes groups do not realize their achievements until someone points them out with a summary. Summaries are also reminders in the sense that they provide a recall of events. They can also help to ensure agreement about events. For example, if during the summary the group leader finds that there are differing perceptions about what has happened, this provides an opportunity to clear up any errors or misunderstandings.

STAGES OF GROUP DEVELOPMENT

In order to understand how group leaders use different attitudes and behaviors during different stages of group development, this section begins with a presentation of the stages. After the presentation of stages, the discussion focuses on leader attitudes and behaviors that are effective and emphasized for each stage. That is, leader tasks differ according to the group's needs and groups' needs vary by stage of development.

I refer often to group stages throughout this book, as many of the concepts and strategies described herein are related to the behaviors, feelings, and attitudes associated with these stages. Studies on group development show that groups move through general sequential stages, although there is no agreement on the number of stages. For example, Tuckman and colleagues identify five stages (Tuckman, 1965; Tuckman and Jensen, 1977), Worchel, Countant-Sassic, and Grassman (1992) propose six stages, and Yalom (1995) defines four stages. The number of stages is not as important as an understanding that groups are expected to change over time in their interactions and progress. For example, both the leader and members are more likely to be able to effectively deal with conflict when they know such conflict is an expected occurrence in the second stage of group development, and that groups who do not allow conflict to emerge or do not constructively resolve it do not move to the cohesive, working, and productive stage.

Table 5.1 presents a summary of expected behaviors, attitudes, and feelings associated with general stages of group development. For our purposes, the stages used are beginning, conflict, cohesion, and termination. Groups will almost always experience beginning, conflict, and termination stages, but can operate without experiencing a cohesion stage. When groups lack a cohesion stage, however, there will be general dissatisfaction with the group and productivity will suffer. Each stage is briefly described below.

Stage 1—Beginning

All groups have a beginning stage. Even when all members have previously worked together, a new project or undertaking is a new beginning for the group. Because the members are familiar with the maintenance functions of the group, such a group will move quickly through the beginning stage, but they still experience many of the same needs as do newly formed groups.

There is always some degree of anxiety present in the beginning stages of groups. For some groups the anxiety is almost overwhelming, while for others, the anxiety is merely uncomfortable. The degree depends on the amount of anxiety experienced by all members in the group collectively. In other words, no one member determines the degree of anxiety for the groups; all members do. This anxiety is displayed by expressions of confusion and frustration, considerable questioning, and requests for more information, direction, and structure. Careful planning can help reduce some anxiety but nothing anyone does can prevent or eliminate it.

Another related characteristic of the beginning stage is the group's search for safety. Members need to feel that they will not be attacked or hurt by participating in the group.

Table 5.1 Expected Member Behaviors and Group Stage

Stage	Group Member Behaviors
Initial	*meeting is invariably a success*
	must achieve purpose or aim and attend to social relationships
	considerable questioning
	confusion between group goals and personal goals
	search for personal viable roles
	search for inclusion
	search for group norms
	search for similarities
	giving and seeking advice
	relatively stereotyped and restricted communication style
Second	*search for dominance*
	a social pecking order emerges
	intermember criticism
	considerable "should" and "ought"
	struggle for control
	hostility toward the leader
	group members may propose a democratic structure
	emergence of rival hostile feelings toward other members
	emergence of displaced, off-target aggression
Third	*consensual group action*
	increased mutual trust
	concerned with intimacy
	greater freedom of self-disclosure
	suppression of negative affect
	attendance improves
Fourth	*devaluing of group experience*
	anxiety reemerges
	panic can set in
	denial of feelings around termination
	irritability and other negative feelings

How do students express these safety needs? The primary way is through questioning the instructor about course requirements and especially about the group requirements. They will ask for the same information in several ways even when it is available on the syllabus. I noticed that students in my class consistently asked for clarification of clearly expressed statements on the syllabus. For several semesters I tried to rewrite requirements so that I would not be asked to further clarify them; I assumed that I had not clearly expressed my expectations. Once I accepted that they were clearly written, I began the practice of briefly reviewing the syllabus in the first class, asking students to read it before the second class, when I would answer questions and clarify anything that was confusing. By the second class, there were hardly any questions and the anxiety level about class expectations was considerably lower. This indicated to me that the requests for clarification and structure were more a manifestation of their anxiety than a real need for more information.

Students also tend to ask for more structure in the beginning stages, and instructors must take care not to buy into their anxiety by trying to give them more and more precision. The task is to provide enough structure so that they can accomplish the goal but not so much structure that creativity and initiative are stifled. Further, an instructor is likely to find that it is impossible to provide enough structure to satisfy everyone.

This is not to say that an instructor should not pay attention to students' requests for more structure. There are times when additional structure is needed in order for the task to be accomplished. But the instructor needs to be aware that some requests for more structure are really a disguised expression of anxiety, and that providing more structure will neither relieve their anxiety nor facilitate accomplishing the task or goal.

Stage 2—Conflict

Conflict typically emerges during this stage. It is very important that the instructor and the group leader be emotionally prepared for this stage so that the conflicts can be dealt with constructively instead of being suppressed or ineffectively resolved. It is also important that the conflict not be ignored or denied, for unless it is allowed to emerge and be constructively resolved, the third stage of cohesion, which is the productive working stage, does not fully develop.

Conflict can be expressed directly or indirectly, mildly or intensely, between members, between members and the leader, and between the group and the instructor. Conflict is not necessarily hostile, however. For example, conflict can occur over a clash of values, cultural differences or expectations, or when dependency or power needs are not met.

Group members may need to be educated about constructive conflict. Many may have the perception that conflict is destructive, especially to relationships, and may avoid expressing differences of opinion or ideas because they fear that having conflicting opinions will be destructive or that they will be attacked for being different. On the other hand, there may be a group member (with luck no more than one in a group) who delights in stirring up conflict and can be counted on to make trouble. Some are so adept that they manage to get other members quarreling while remaining on the outside themselves. These conflicts can indeed be destructive and must be prevented or blocked.

A struggle for power and control is also expected in stage 2, especially when many students are competitive or when the task demands competition. Competition can make it difficult for some to work collaboratively or cooperatively, as everything seems a competition and everyone a competitor.

Many students will deny to themselves or others their competitiveness and/or need for power and control. They may perceive these characteristics as aggressive and do not want to be perceived as aggressive. What they may fail to realize is that these characteristics are present in everyone but differ in intensity and kind, and do not always signal aggressiveness. For example, the person who wants to know all the specifics before attempting something new or unfamiliar has some reasonable level of need for control. The person who micromanages, on the other hand, has a strong need for control that may be unreasonable.

Power and control needs, even if mild in nature, can emerge in the group and fuel conflict. What students, and perhaps the instructor, should realize is that these needs should be recognized and not allowed to undermine the functioning of the group by being denied or ignored.

Stage 3—Cohesion

When groups successfully work through conflicts, cohesion results. Members learn that conflicts do not mean that relationships or the self are destroyed but that stronger bonds between the persons involved can emerge. Cohesive groups are characterized by mutual respect and caring among members, cooperation, and productivity. Whatever the work of the group may be, members work hard to ensure accomplishment.

Stage 3 is not an all-or-nothing stage. Conflict lessens, but may not entirely disappear. However, members may suppress some personal negative feelings because the overall feelings in the group are positive. They seem more willing to tolerate minor discomfort because the group is going so well. If, on the other hand, they feel some intense emotion such as anger, they are more willing to try to work through it and the conflict because their experience in stage 2 has given them confidence in themselves and in their ability to effect a positive outcome.

Groups in this stage assume more initiative and need less leading and directing. Both the group leader and the instructor can function as consultants.

The work for the group gets accomplished and members have positive feelings about themselves, the group, and their work.

Stage 4—Termination

All groups end, but too many times termination is not planned for. When the group is stopped without an acknowledgment of its ending or a process for ending that takes into account members' feelings about the group and its accomplishments, the group experience feels truncated.

Both the instructor and the group leader should stay aware of the life span for the group and begin planning how to terminate the group approximately halfway through its life span. Satisfactory termination depends on the personality and needs of group members; there is no one way for ending. The primary components for successful termination are awareness of time left for the group work, conscious decisions about constructive use of that time, reflection on the experience, and expressing feelings.

One caution: termination should be focused on the group's ending and not turned into a social event. Members will suggest a party or some sort of celebration. This is appropriate when separated from the process of termination. They can have the event after the last group session but not as a substitute for the session. The social event should not be used as a way to ignore or deny feelings about termination.

Group Stage Overview

Instructors and group leaders should remember that each stage is not clearly delineated, nor can members' behaviors at each stage always be clearly understood except in retrospect. That is, it may be difficult to immediately identify the group's stage by individual members' behaviors; a focus on the group is a more useful indicator. For example, a member's challenge of the leader in the first few sessions does not mean the group is in stage 2. If, on the other hand, several group members express dissatisfaction with how the group is progressing after it has been in operation for some time, and tend to snipe at each other and the leader, then the group is most likely in stage 2.

Groups cannot be pushed arbitrarily from one stage to another, except to termination. Even then, however, pushing will not be effective if the group is determined to resist. Leaders and the instructor must understand that groups develop at their own pace over time. It is important to allow this to happen, facilitate the process, and not be anxious when the group does not appear to be moving from one stage to another.

Table 5.2 presents leader attitudes and behaviors that facilitate group development and task accomplishment. Stage 1 is characterized by attitudes to reduce fear and anxiety, and by very active behaviors. The group leader has

**Table 5.2 Leader Attitudes and Behaviors and
Group Developmental Stages**

Attitudes	Behaviors
Stage 1	
Belief in efficacy of group	Directing, concreteness, selling, encouraging, stimulating, explaining, clarifying, setting limits, caring, protecting, active listening and responding
Anxiety is expected (self and members)	
Genuineness	
Warmth	
Positive regard	
Nonjudgmental	
Acceptance	
Empathy	
Stage 2	
Conflict is expected	Less directing, more focus on experiencing here and now, facilitating conflict resolution, confronting, challenging, active listening and responding, blocking
Lack of defensiveness	
Understand competitiveness	
Risk-taking	
Empathy	
Stage 3	
Members will work independently	Little directing, functioning as a consultant, supporting, praising, active listening and responding
Empathy	
Stage 4	
Termination is a process and must be planned and experienced	Remind of group's ending, attend to relationships, assist members in determining how they will terminate the group, active listening and responding
Empathy	

to be very attentive and organized at the beginning of group, which can be difficult for beginning group leaders as they tend to be inexperienced.

Attitudes and behaviors in stage 2 revolve around conflict and conflict resolution. Anticipating the emergence of conflict and having specific strategies to assist in mediating and constructive conflict resolution give the group leader confidence that conflict will not necessarily be destructive. This confidence is conveyed to group members and they become more comfortable with their ability to contain and manage conflict. They learn conflict resolution strategies that can be used in other settings, especially in real-world work settings.

Groups that reach stage 3 need very little from the group leader. This is when the group leader should back off, be less active, have confidence in the group's ability to manage its affairs, and serve as a consultant. This can be difficult for those who are accustomed to being active and are inclined to micromanage. Leaders need to learn how to "let go."

Stage 4 is when panic and anxiety can reemerge. Group members become anxious about completing the task and ending the group. There is a tendency to skip over the process for ending and focus on the future instead of the present. The group leader has the task of managing the anxiety and helping members plan for the group's ending. Even when the group experience was not the most comfortable or productive, there should be a period for reflecting on the experience and evaluating outcomes.

SUMMARY

Work for the group leader is extensive, but so is the learning. This person not only gains knowledge about the class content but also learns new ways of managing work and people. Group leaders have an opportunity to learn organizational, relationship, and communication skills that have real-life applications. They are introduced to group dynamics and process, and can gain an understanding of the power and efficacy of group work. This experience can help build confidence in their ability to lead groups, as well as promoting "faith" in the group work. The instructor who invests the time to prepare a group leader carefully will reap the rewards of both effective groups and successful students.

CHAPTER 6

Conflict: Inevitable and Manageable

Consulting any dictionary produces various definitions for *conflict:* struggle, battle, disagreement, dispute, quarrel, opposition, collision, difference, discord, and contest. In psychology, *conflict* is defined as the opposition or simultaneous functioning of mutually exclusive impulses, desires, or tendencies. Thus, conflict can occur within an individual, between persons, or between groups. Conflicts can range from mild (to differ) to intense (to battle or collide), with many stops between. In short, there are numerous kinds of conflict and none of them are escapable.

Once the inescapability of conflict is understood, it becomes easier to understand that conflict will surface in all groups. The nature and kind will differ, but it is unrealistic to expect any group to function without some sort of conflict. All group leaders should be prepared for conflict to occur; what follows are some suggestions for how to deal with it.

There are four major suggestions: increase awareness of personal reactions; distinguish between constructive and destructive conflict; become sensitive to the varying reactions of group members; and be prepared to recognize conflict.

The first thing that any group leader should take into account is his or her personal reaction to conflict. For some the very thought is upsetting and frightening. Others perceive conflict as a contest and want to enter the fray. Most are somewhere between the two extremes. This self-awareness is important because the group leader will model and teach conflict resolution or conflict suppression.

The second point is that conflict can be either destructive or constructive to the group. The group leader will play an important part in determining if the conflict positively or negatively affects relationships and productivity, again, by modeling and teaching about conflict.

The third point is that the group leader needs to become sensitive to the many levels and intensity of group members' reactions to conflict. The extreme reaction to conflict may be a result of faulty perceptions that conflict is abusive and destructive, and so milder forms, such as differences and challenges, may be overlooked or ignored until they become more open clashes.

Finally, the group leader should expect that conflict will occur between him or her and the members. This is characteristic of stage two of group development, when the members challenge the leader in some way. How such challenges are handled by the leader sets the tone for how other conflicts will be handled in the group and how confident the group leader is, and can model an effective way of dealing with conflict.

LEVELS OF EXTERNAL CONFLICT

External conflicts are those between people, such as a conflict between the leader and the group or between group members. Proposed are four levels of external conflict, ranging from mild to intense. Each is briefly defined and described.

Level 1 conflicts are mild and result from differences between people that are not fully understood. For example, members may have a conflict over when to hold group meetings because some members work or have transportation problems that other members do not have. Until these differences are ironed out, the members are in a mild conflict. Some conflicts of interest, values, and needs fall at this level because such qualities help define a person, but do not usually produce considerable emotional intensity unless another person disparages or discounts them in some way.

Level 2 conflicts are a little more serious in that emotions are more intense. This is the level where interests collide, disputes occur, and disagreements escalate. Irritations and annoyances can build up if not openly discussed. An example of level 2 conflict is when a decision-making process does not include all members and so some feel pushed or railroaded. Members are increasingly likely to disagree and may begin to label each other with terms such as *dominating* or *pushy.*

Level 3 conflicts emerge because of clashes of deeply held values, or when members feel attacked or deeply wounded. For example, those sensitive about being excluded and those whose input is not solicited, may become deeply wounded, and begin to promote conflict. Conflicts at this level can be very destructive to individuals and to the group.

Level 4 conflicts have so much emotion connected to them that they are most likely to become destructive to members. The group is angry, members feel frightened, and verbal abuse escalates. The group leader is crucial in making sure that the group does not reach this level.

RECOGNIZING CONFLICT

A group leader has to develop the ability to recognize when conflict emerges. Some conflicts are easy to identify: the participants openly disagree, dispute, clash, or quarrel. More difficult to identify are conflicts that are hidden, suppressed, or denied. Further, a leader's characteristic way of dealing with conflict may be to ignore it or smooth it over; however, if conflict is not allowed to emerge and members do not engage in constructive conflict resolution, the problem will eat away at the group.

This is not to say that every time there is a disagreement the leader needs to resolve it; that would be time-consuming and unproductive. Some disagreements disappear on their own, as individuals realize that they are displacing feelings and moods from the outside onto the group. When those conditions are resolved or changed, their group behavior changes and they no longer feel a need to disagree or quarrel. For example, if a member had a dispute with a friend prior to the group session, she may still be fuming and easily irritated in the session. The next session finds her over these feelings, and much more cooperative. The important thing for the group leader to realize is when it is necessary for him or her to intervene.

DISGUISED, MASKED, OR REPRESSED CONFLICT

Conflict that is in some way hidden from the group or even the individual experiencing it can have the most negative impact on the group and manifest itself in unexpected ways. This kind of conflict is very difficult to identify, even for experienced group leaders, and many times is only dimly sensed. Its hidden and denied nature also makes it unlikely that it can be brought to the group's attention and constructively resolved or mediated. Further, the nature of internal conflicts is so complex and personal that it is not usually appropriate to try to work through or with them in the context of a classroom group.

An example of a hidden conflict and how it can impact the group illustrates just how difficult they can be. It is not uncommon to have one or more group members who will not openly express their personal preferences, opinions, or ideas if they appear to be different from one or more other members in the group. It is a conflict because they disagree or differ, and the conflict is hidden because they do not speak. So, not realizing that the conflict exists, the rest of the group proceeds as if everyone were in agreement. Decisions are made and tasks assigned based on the false assumption that all members have bought into or are committed to the decision. The leader feels that the group is progressing and the project is underway. It probably does not take long for frustration to set in, however, because for some reason, nothing much is being accomplished. Minor irritations about nonessential matters that were previously ignored or worked out now begin to consume much of the group's time.

Decisions are constantly resisted and revised. Group members are testy and dissatisfied but no amount of exploration seems to make a difference.

The above scenario is all too common an outcome for unexpressed conflict. This is one reason why some group experiences produce antipathy or reluctance on the part of some members to engage in further group or team work. Just imagine how difficult it must be for a group leader faced with a "secret" situation that is retarding the group's development and progress.

Hidden, masked, or repressed conflicts occur when a group member or members:

- Fear rejection if they disagree or differ
- Want to be accepted and so tend to agree with everything
- Are skeptical of the leader's ability or competence
- Wish that a member or leader would shut up
- Struggle to connect or understand
- Keep quiet when they dissent
- Compete indirectly for attention, affection, power, or control
- Fear to challenge a position, idea, or person

The group leader may not recognize any or some of these as conflicts and therefore, will not make appropriate interventions. It takes increased awareness and experience to learn how to recognize this class of conflicts and to know when and how to intervene.

DECIDING TO INTERVENE

Leader intervention is indicated when:

- Group members become polarized or take sides
- A member is on the verge of being made a scapegoat
- An active participant falls silent
- Members are attacking each other verbally
- The leader is aware of suppressed conflict that is affecting the group's progress

Polarized Members

This is one of the more obvious manifestations of conflict in a group. Members become polarized around a value or principle and suddenly, whatever the topic, the same collection of members rally to the same position and voice agreement over and over.

For example, suppose that a classroom discussion group addresses current events. Welfare reform generates considerable discussion and disputes around racial issues. One subgroup maintains that although race has nothing to do with their position, their principles are that people should have to work for a living and should not look to the government for their support and livelihood, and that poor Blacks and Hispanics are just not trying hard enough to get out of poverty. They quote many references in support of their position. The other subgroup contends that this position is prejudiced and racially biased. It gets to the point where even trying to have a discussion about the advantages and disadvantages of elected school board mayors and other city officials elicits the same arguments from the subgroups, neither of which changes their position in the slightest degree.

Cliques are one reason why members of a subgroup consistently support each other. In such cases, the only real "principle" involved is the one that defines who is in the subgroup and therefore to be supported and agreed with, and who is not in the subgroup, and therefore is wrong. It will not make any difference what the topic is; if someone in the clique takes a position or defines a preference, he or she can count on one or more others to agree and support. This kind of conflict can be difficult to identify at first, because cliques can take time to develop and be recognized. But, if an existing relationship between two or more group members is already known, the leader needs to take steps to keep a clique from developing, starting at the beginning group session.

The pattern of communication is the best clue to identify when polarization or taking sides is occurring. Observe which members usually or consistently agree with each other, rescue or support each other, and tend not to voice differing opinions or ideas. This kind of conflict is usually minor, and can be quickly and directly worked out between the individuals with little direction from the leader.

Scapegoating

Conflict in the group can be manifested by the group's scapegoating of one or more members. When the group decides that a particular member is not meeting some expectation and start pointing the finger of blame at him or her, this person becomes the repository of all of the group's frustration and anger. The scapegoat is a target, and also a diversion from what may be more serious underlying group problems.

It does not help in identification of the conflict that the "target" is exhibiting some of the attitude and behaviors of which he or she are accused. Further, by scapegoating this person the group deflects attention from other more significant and, perhaps hidden, conflicts.

The group will be more effective if the scapegoating behavior is blocked by the leader and the group helped to better define the other hidden conflicts in the group. Rescuing the scapegoated members is secondary. In addition, blocking by the leader (described in Chapter 7) will probably not make other members ashamed or guilty for their scapegoating.

Falling Silent

Another signal of conflict is when a member who has been verbally active falls silent. He or she may be suppressing an open disagreement or dispute, and reluctant to say anything for fear it will promote conflict. Or perhaps the person was attacked or felt attacked when voicing a position or opinion. Either way, someone's falling silent may indicate unspoken conflict in the group, especially if the group norm is that conflict must be suppressed and avoided. Unfortunately, this will hamper and retard the progress and productivity of the group.

A group leader who notices a silent member may want to say, "I notice that you have become somewhat quieter in this session and I wonder what is causing you to be quiet." This gives the person an opportunity to talk about their reasons for falling silent. Quite often, however, the person will deny any particular reason and the group leader then has to reflect on recent group events and try to identify what happened. If the conflict is disguised, the leader's intervention may be needed to help the group recognize and constructively deal with it.

Verbal Attacks

This can be the most visible and easily identified form of conflict in the group. Few, if any, doubt that there is conflict when verbal attacks are direct and overt. However, verbal attacks can also be indirect and disguised, and hence less easily recognized. Further, these attacks are not just between members, they also occur between the group and the leader. Conflict between the group and the leader is the conflict that most often goes unidentified or ignored although it is one that can be predicted.

Member-to-member verbal attacks are often the result of accumulated irritations and annoyances. Feelings are suppressed until they build up and explode as a verbal attack. Note also that a verbal attack does not always have raised voices to carry considerable effect. Harsh words do not need to be shouted, and some people are adept at concealing the level and intensity of their feelings.

Verbal attacks can also be the outcome of displaced anger. That is, the attacker is really angry at someone else, even someone outside the group, but has chosen to displace the anger onto another group member. This displacement is usually not done consciously, which makes it difficult for either the leader or the attacker to recognize.

Leaders need to track both indirect and disguised verbal attacks, especially those directed at themselves. Constructive interventions cannot be implemented if the conflict goes unidentified and unacknowledged.

Suppressed Conflict

The term *suppressed conflict* means that members are aware that they disagree but choose not to do so in an open and direct way. They "sit on" their feelings in order to maintain harmony or ensure that conflict does not emerge. Members have many reasons for suppressing their feelings. Some may fear that if they say what they feel or want, they will offend others in some way or be ignored or rejected. They find many ways of justifying the suppression, rationalizing that the time is not right, or that they would be seen as different or odd, or that it is not worth the effort. The end result is that these feelings are not dealt with or dispersed, continue to build up, and begin to affect the group's progress.

Suppressed conflict can emerge in many ways. Members feel that the group is stuck, become bored, or find ways not to participate. The longer they engage in this behavior, the more intense the feelings become and the more likely they are to emerge in a destructive way. Little things become annoying and members become more willing to be critical of each other and the leader. There is a general air of dissatisfaction in the group, making it difficult for all concerned.

Leaders can facilitate progression through stage 2 of group development by encouraging members to express the conflict(s) more openly and directly. The group will not reach the working stage, stage 3, until members deal with the suppressed conflict.

MINOR OR MAJOR CONFLICT?

Sometimes it can be difficult to decide if the conflict is a major one or if it is minor and can be safely ignored. A group leader should not assume that a conflict is minor because the content appears trivial or because the feelings expressed do not appear to be intense. Sometimes what appears to be minor is just the tip of the iceberg, and ignoring it ensures that the group will founder on it in the future. The group leader will learn through experience how and when to judge the severity of a conflict.

Novice group leaders may wish to check out their hunches about conflicts with the group. They can say something like, "It seems to me that there is some disagreement about _____," and ask for confirmation from the group. If there appears to be conflict between two or more members, the leader can ask both parties, "How important is this for you?" and be guided not only by the verbal response but also by the tone of voice and quality of feeling displayed. Noticing all of these allows the leader to better judge if the conflict is major and needs immediate attention, or if it is minor and can be delayed or ignored.

BASIC GUIDELINES FOR LEADERS IN CONFLICT INTERVENTION

Once it becomes necessary for the leader to intervene, some basic guidelines for engaging in conflict resolution or conflict mediation must be considered:

- Listen
- Remain neutral
- Delay when appropriate
- Intervene early
- Let both sides win
- Use active listening skills

Each is briefly discussed.

Listen

The group leader should always listen to both sides and try not to let preferences or personalities influence his or her behavior. The leader, of course, is entitled to a personal opinion, but should adopt an attitude of neutrality if the intervention is to be successful. If either party senses that the leader has already come to a decision, then any intervention is doomed to fail and relationships will be harmed.

Remain Neutral

Being neutral means not openly taking sides, regardless of whether one side is more appealing or appears to be more correct than the other. If the leader takes sides, then the side not favored feels rejected by the powerful authority figure and begins to wonder if it has a place in the group. Then the leader will have to overcome these negative feelings in addition to the conflict.

Delay When Appropriate

Delay intervention when feelings are too intense, for they may intensify after you begin the process for resolution, mediation, or concinnity. Emotional intensity usually signals heightened sensitivity and reduced rationality, objectivity, and ability to listen accurately. For example, an angry or hurt person finds it difficult to accept that the other person has a valid point or position.

The angry one cannot accurately "hear and understand" what the other is trying to communicate. When this happens, there is an increased chance of misunderstanding added to the existing conflict.

Intervene Early

It can be helpful and instructive to try and work out small conflicts early in the group, for early intervention can prevent escalation and promote feelings of safety. That is, members see early on that it is possible to deal with conflicts in a constructive way and that the group leader is competent and not afraid of conflict.

Let Both Sides Win

Crucial to constructively working out conflicts is that both parties should somehow "win." Few, if any, people like to lose and it can take some time to overcome the resentment, anger, or hurt that accompanies losing. Further, group members can begin to adopt the attitude and norm that the group will have winners and losers, which is not desirable.

The group leader takes the lead in assuming that it is possible for both parties to "win." It will be difficult for anyone enmeshed in the conflict to take this attitude, so the group leader must commit to working out a solution that allows both parties to gain and not to go away feeling like losers.

Use Active Listening Skills

Active listening and reflecting are crucial skills. Added to this is the need to listen for misperceptions or wrong information. Chapter 9 describes active listening and how to develop the skill. When engaging in conflict resolution or mediation, a group leader needs to make a special effort to use these skills, for it is crucial that each party in the conflict feels heard and understood. The leader will be trusted more when both parties can rely on his or her understanding of the issues and emotions in the conflict and attention to the process.

An important part of listening is attending, discussed more extensively in Chapter 9. Attending by the listener makes the speaker feel that what he or she has to say is important. In this way, the group leader can inspire trust in the parties of the conflict and set the stage for all to truly hear what is said and meant. Attending also helps to better focus on body posture and gestures that can signal the degree of the speaker's emotional intensity. This helps the leader to better judge when to delay, back off, or continue to discuss the conflict.

Two more major components of active listening that are helpful in conflict situations are reflection and paraphrasing. Reflection is the act of mirroring what was said and meant. Paraphrasing is repeating what was said by rephrasing it. Reflection involves both content and feelings, while paraphrasing uses just the content. These are skills to be developed and practiced so that they can be smoothly done, without sounding like a parrot.

One final aspect of listening, for this discussion, is that in order to listen, the leader must be quiet. One cannot listen and talk at the same time. Because we can think faster than we can talk, it is sometimes difficult to sit quietly while someone else is talking. This is one reason why interruptions and completing someone else's sentences occur. Listening, however, means resisting the urge to do either of these. This can be particularly difficult when someone seems to be groping for words, or talking around the topic. Still, one must be quiet in order to listen; listening effectively is one of a leader's most important tools.

A Strategy and Process for Conflict Resolution

This section focuses on a specific strategy and process for intervening in conflicts. It can be termed conflict resolution or mediation, and is intended to guide the novice group leader. It may be helpful for an instructor to put the list of steps in Table 6.1 in the guidelines for group leaders and for the student leaders to memorize the steps. Why memorize? Because some conflicts can emerge unexpectedly and require immediate interventions; the leader will not have time to look up the process, but must act on the spot to be effective. In other words, do not wait until the next session to intervene, unless emotions are too intense or there is not enough time to even begin to start the process.

Each of the steps in the conflict intervention process is briefly discussed below.

Table 6.1   Steps in the Conflict Intervention Process

1.	Act as quickly as possible
2.	Identify issues
3.	Defuse affect
4.	Require restatement of the other position
5.	Establish goals
6.	Determine flexibility of parties
7.	Propose alternatives
8.	Explore advantages and disadvantages of alternatives
9.	Involve group members not in conflict
10.	Select a solution

Act as Quickly as Possible

Timing the intervention close to when an overt conflict emerges is important. If left to fester, conflict can negatively affect the group's functioning. Further, sometimes one of the parties will want to deny the conflict; immediate identification of the conflict allows the group leader to explain his or her conclusion while behaviors are still fresh in everyone's minds.

Action for a covert conflict does not have to be immediate, especially since it may not even be recognized until some time later when reflecting on past sessions. In this instance, the leader should say to the group that he or she has become aware that there is a conflict and then go on to provide evidence to support the conclusion, which should be based primarily on observable behaviors. Input from other group members should also be solicited to support the contention that there is conflict.

Identify Issues

It is the group leader's responsibility to identify major issues in the conflict for both sides. The leader's goal is to state concisely the bone of contention, using only content at this point.

Identification of issues takes place by listening to what is said, trying to identify essential elements and feelings, and paying attention to the intensity of feelings. While the leader should not point out feelings at this time, they are important as clues to the importance of an issue. To pick out the major issues from all a member is saying can be difficult, but noting the greatest intensity of feelings tells you that this is what is most important.

Defuse Affect

It is not unusual for intense emotions to be connected to a conflict. One or both parties will feel strongly about their positions and can become incensed if they feel threatened, not respected, or not heard. A group leader should be very aware that these intense emotions will affect not only the parties involved in the conflict, but also the other group members.

What, specifically, can the leader do to defuse the affect? First, acknowledge the importance of each party's position. This conveys to each that the leader is aware that this conflict is not trivial or inconsequential.

Second, ask for an explanation or clarification of the extent of the importance for each party. The leader may think he or she knows why it is so important, but may also often be wrong. It is better not to assume, but to make sure everyone truly understands.

Third, if either or both parties are intensely emotionally involved, note this. Just say that you notice that they seem to feel intensely about the situation. Allow each side to express its viewpoint without interruption. Tell them that this is the group procedure, and ask for their cooperation. Even if one side wants to correct an error or misperception, it must wait until the other side has finished. Use alphabetical order to determine who presents first and explain that this is the process.

Finally, do not agree or disagree with anything—simply reflect what was said. The leader may need to correct any misperceptions or facts if they are important—particularly if there would be no conflict if the member had the correct facts—but otherwise delay any corrections. It is best if the leader can remain as neutral as possible at this point.

Require Restatement of the Other Position

It is very helpful to have each party restate the other's position or issue to make sure that all participants are hearing and understanding the same thing. Further, by having them do the restating, the leader ensures that each side has at least heard the other party, and allows for clarification of any misunderstandings and correction of any facts. Restating should continue until the leader and the other party agree that the review is correct.

Establish Goals

The leader is in a position to help both parties in a conflict establish goals or desired outcomes; that is, what would be a satisfying resolution for each? This may take some time, as each is likely to want to "win." However, by having them state what they consider to be a satisfying resolution, the leader at least has something to begin to work toward. Ideally, the leader can get both sides to agree on mutual goals.

Determine Flexibility of Parties

This is often accomplished simultaneously with establishing goals. Determine how flexible each party will be about giving up a piece of its position. A leader can get some sense of this while each is talking about desired outcomes, but may need to ask directly what accommodations they are willing to make, which gets them thinking about what is and isn't subject to compromise in their position.

If either, or both, parties describe themselves as inflexible, do not challenge them or try to get them to change their mind right now. Return to the question after completing some of the other steps. It is not crucial at this point to get a commitment to compromise.

Propose Alternatives

As a leader listens to the parties present their positions and desired outcomes, he or she may develop alternatives for them to consider. It is important that these not be presented as orders or dictates. Ask if they have considered these ideas, or if they are willing to talk about the pros and cons. The leader's goal is to get them to think about how to resolve the conflict, and not to stick in one position with no possibility of change or movement.

The leader may also bring other members into the discussion by opening the floor to suggestions and alternatives for resolution from the group. Do not let other members start to take sides; block any and all of this behavior. Just say to someone who starts to support one or the other party, "It would be helpful if you could give some alternatives at this point."

Explore Advantages and Disadvantages

After brainstorming some possible alternatives, focus on the pros and cons for each. It is important not to quickly jump to a resolution but to carefully consider the advantages and disadvantages of each. What may, at first glance, appear to be a promising solution can have too many hidden problems. Do not take too much time in exploring, but do not leave out this step.

Involve Group Members

Some of the previous steps have noted that group members not directly involved in the conflict can help in resolution. If, to this point, other group members have not been directly included in the discussion, they should now be brought in and their opinions and feelings solicited. These other members were actively participating even if they did not say anything, and may be carrying intense feelings that need to be processed. Make them a part of the solution.

Select a Solution

This is the point at which conflicting parties agree to a mutual solution, which is often a compromise that calls for each to give up something. The group leader should not force a solution, just provide an opportunity for the participants to select one. Care should be taken that the agreement is real and not just a way to get the whole thing over with and to take the spotlight off those involved.

CHAPTER 7

Problem Behaviors and Interventions

Problem behaviors can surface in many groups, and all groups can expect some problem behavior, even if only temporary and easily resolved. Careful planning by the instructor, a complete syllabus, and detailed guidelines can help reduce or prevent many problem behaviors, such as absenteeism, but there are other, less predictable problem behaviors that cannot be treated this way.

Following are some common behaviors that can present problems for the group:

- Silence
- Monopolizing
- Hostility
- Rescuing
- Socializing
- Poor performance
- Irresponsible behavior
- Inattentiveness
- Harassment
- Aggressiveness (Corey & Corey, 1998; Gazda et al., 1995; Gladding, 1995)

Few novice group leaders, if any, are prepared to effectively handle these, and many will just ignore them without realizing their negative impact on the group. Some behaviors will be handled by chastising the member, thereby alienating that member and making other members fear that they too will be chastised or criticized. Problem behaviors can be handled by a leader who has some notion of what to expect and how to handle them. Table 7.1 presents

Table 7.1   Problem Behaviors and Possible Goals/Reasons

Problem Behaviors	Possible Goals/Reasons
Silence	Escape conflict
	Avoid involvement
	Want to be encouraged
	Punish leader/members
	Can't form a response
	Avoid self-disclosure
	Shyness
Monopolizing	Be center of attention
	Avoid attacks, criticism
	Want to be fully understood
	Want to avoid violation
	Dislike or uncomfortable with silence
Hostility	Avoid being hurt by others
	Seek revenge
	Deflect attention from personal faults
	Dissatisfaction with self, life circumstances
Rescuing	Suppress threatening feeling
	Keep the environment "safe"
	Want to be perceived positively
Socializing	Unwillingness to work on task (resistance)
	Want to be liked
	Insecurity about abilities
	Confusion about what is expected
	Desire to be "included"
	Seek to promote harmony
Poor Performance	Personal problems
	Overcommitment
	Poor time management skills
	Poor instructions or guidelines received
	Inability to do the work
	Feel "excluded"
	Illness
Irresponsible Behavior	Immaturity
	Personal problems
	Unexpected crises
	Feeling "excluded"
	Poor communication among members

(Continued)

Table 7.1 (*Continued*)

Problem Behaviors	Possible Goals/Reasons
Inattentiveness	Illness
	Personal problems
	Boredom
	Environment
	Hostility
Harassment	Insecurity
	Feeling of superiority
	Entitlement
	Manipulation
	Contempt
	Ignorance of policies
Aggressiveness	Domination
	Power needs
	Hostility
	Feeling of superiority

some problem behaviors and the following discussion presents some clues for identifying them. The remainder of the chapter presents some strategies group leaders can use.

PROBLEM BEHAVIORS

Silence

A member who is silent, speaking only when directly asked to do so will, at some point, become a problem for the group, as the leader and other members will begin to feel that this person is not interested in or committed to the group. Others will become irritated at having to draw out this person and will resent having to make the effort.

The other kind of silence that can be a problem occurs when a member who was actively participating suddenly falls silent. The leader and other group members wonder what happened to cause him or her to stop actively participating. Some may even wonder if they did or said something that was offensive.

Both situations detract from the group because the behavior troubles the leader and members in some way. Thus, they are distracted from the task and other group members.

Monopolizing

The person who talks a lot, tells stories, rambles, goes off on a tangent, or otherwise consumes much of the group's time is demonstrating monopolizing behavior. At first, the group leader may be grateful for the active participation and other members relieved that someone else is keeping the session moving. But it is not long before everyone wishes this person would shut up or stay focused. A group leader needs to prevent this behavior without alienating the person or scaring other members.

At times a monopolizer may bring personal concerns to the group, and members will want to be caring and sympathetic. Worse is when members then start trying to give advice or solve the problem. Any attempt to cut the member off will be viewed as cold and uncaring. This presents a dilemma for the leader, as group time is being used unproductively but trying to get back on track will make members resent the leader; everyone ends up frustrated.

Hostility

The angry, hostile person can arouse anger, hostility, or fear in others. Hostile people are characterized by loud rapid speech (Tavris, 1982), body tension, and a litany of complaints. They appear to be constantly on guard and are quick to take offense. These people perceive practically everything and everyone as a potential threat or attack.

Worse for the group are those who are passively hostile or who are adept at masking their hostility. These people are sociable and cooperative—on the surface. It is only over time that others become aware of the extent of their hostility.

Both forms of hostility affect the group. While members, including the leader, can recognize the hostile person, they may be less apt to be aware of their own responses to the hostility and how it is affecting their participation in group. The leader and members also find themselves being very careful in expression because they fear arousing overt or covert hostility from that member. The passive hostile person may cloak their hostility in sarcasm or jokes making it difficult for others to directly confront them. After all, few people are comfortable with being considered humorless or unable to take a joke.

Rescuing

Helping someone who appears to be in distress or having difficulty is a common and helpful response. However, if a member is working through a problem and sorting through feelings, and is assisted too much or too soon, learning and growth can be truncated. Much like the caterpillar becoming a butterfly, some struggle is necessary.

Instructors and group leaders must find a delicate balance between giving needed help and rescuing. One does not want to withhold needed help or information, but neither does one want to provide so much that growth and development are retarded.

This needed balance is most apparent during the beginning stages of group where students are anxious and frustrated with ambiguity and ask for or demand more structure. If too much structure is given, creativity and initiative can be stifled, and students will not learn how to deal with the anxiety common in a new situation. On the other hand, there may well be missing information The trick for instructors and leaders is to mentally step back and objectively assess the amount of assistance that is really necessary.

Socializing

Socializing becomes a problem when it supersedes the group's task and maintenance functions. At first, socializers appear to be helpful because they are cheerful and outgoing, reduce tension, and engage other members. However, some members can get so caught up in socializing that they begin to have a negative impact on the group.

This socializing can be especially frustrating when the members form a clique, which is a subgroup of the group. Other members are not included and feel alienated and resentful, which leads to conflict, either overt or covert.

Another type of socializer wants to talk about there-and-then topics, such as movies, sports, or outside relationships, rather than here-and-now task-related group topics. These members usually chatter away either to the entire group or to one or two members, distracting some or even all the group members. If they are tolerated, other group members become exasperated with them, the group, and the leader. If they are attacked, they attack in return or become sullen and withdraw. Further, even the mildest chiding can be perceived as an attack, making everyone feel less safe in the group.

Poor Performance

When tasks are not completed or are done incorrectly, the productivity of the group suffers as do the relationships between members. After all, for most classroom groups, their grades are somewhat dependent on everyone else in the group. When even one person does not, or cannot, live up to the agreement and expectations, all pay the penalty.

The effects of poor performance on the group cannot be ignored or underestimated. Members can become angry, confused, frustrated, and anxious and begin to displace these feelings onto each other, the leader, and/or the instructor. Squabbles and fights break out between members who, up to that point, were cheerful and cooperative. Other members become withdrawn and begin to miss meetings or arrive late. Those who try to compensate for others' poor performance may feel exploited, betrayed, or unappreciated, and in turn become critical of group members—not a happy state of affairs.

Irresponsible Behavior Contrasted with Responsible Behavior

Responsible behavior contributes much to the productivity and functioning of the group. Responsibility includes dependability, dutifulness, awareness of ethical, legal, and moral issues and related behaviors, attentiveness to task, and initiative.

Responsible behavior implies maturity. Group members will have varying degrees of maturity, and so it is reasonable to expect that some irresponsible behavior will exist in almost every group.

Why is responsibility so critical to the group's productivity and functioning? A short description for each characteristic listed above points out the importance.

Dependability means that one can be counted on to keep one's word, be cooperative, and be prompt in accomplishing tasks or meeting expectations. This characteristic also implies a lack of impulsiveness and distractibility, and a willingness to subordinate personal needs for group needs.

Dutifulness means an attention to duty, a willingness to put work before pleasure. The dutiful person considers his or her duty to be more important than fun, at least in the short term.

Awareness of ethical, legal, and moral issues and behaving in a way that supports normative or expected criteria is also very important. The responsible person knows what behaviors are right and wrong, good and bad, and legal and illegal, and governs behavior accordingly. For classroom groups this can be particularly important when groups meet and function independently of the instructor.

The responsible member is attentive to the task and focuses on what is needed to accomplish it. Distractibility is low in this person. Like some of the other characteristics, attentiveness to task means that the person has internalized and adopted behaviors that characterize a mature adult. These attitudes and behaviors are valued in the workplace, promote group productivity, and enhance relationships in the group. They also serve as a model for less mature group members.

Responsible group members will also display initiative. They do not sit back and complain, but rather seek out what is needed, whether it be information, resources, or expertise. They do not fret about things not being given to them; they make their needs known and also act on them. This behavior provides considerable assistance to the group in accomplishing its task and facilitates the development of relationships.

Inattentiveness

Almost every group member can be inattentive at some point in the group life span. It is only when a member is consistently inattentive that behavior becomes disruptive and presents a problem. Inattention robs the group of time; the leader and members become frustrated at having to constantly ask for the dreamers' attention and at having to stop the group to brief them on what occurred during the time they were "elsewhere."

Harassment

Harassment of any type is detrimental to a group and a violation of policies at almost every college and university in the United States. Harassment creates a chilly or hostile climate, not only for the member who is harassed, but also for other group members. Harassment shows hostility and contempt and seeks to demean and disparage. Harassing behaviors include:

- Sexually explicit or inferred jokes and remarks
- Racially offensive jokes and remarks
- Gender-offensive jokes and remarks
- Threatening, intimidating, or aggressive actions
- Touching that is not invited or wanted

Harassment usually is not based on a single remark or action, but is a pattern of behavior over time. However, it is possible for a leader to set a tone for the group by tolerating a single remark, action, or joke that could become a pattern of behavior. Instructors and group leaders should review their institution's policies on harassment and have a statement about it on their syllabus. Students need to learn what is considered harassment so that they can behave in an appropriate manner both in academia and in the workplace.

Aggressiveness

Aggressiveness is not synonymous with violence, although violence is one kind of aggressive behavior. Aggressive behavior can be verbal and emotional abusiveness, or physical nonverbal actions, especially when the intent is to dominate or demonstrate power over another person.

Powerful and assertive people can sometimes appear aggressive to some, especially if the observer is somewhat shy or timid. However, over time their behavior and intent is understood as a part of their personality, with no agenda to dominate or demonstrate power over others. These are not the people who present problems to the group.

Those who do present problems are the bullies, intimidators, narcissists, sociopaths, etc. Their goal is manipulation of others through fear that, in turn, provides them with a sense of superiority, power, control, and domination.

This sort of behavior can destroy a group even when the aggression does not become violent. Members dread saying anything that may bring on the aggressive behavior and make them a target. They also fear that being quiet will cause the person to consider them a target, so they fear being a target if they say something or if they do not say anything. It is a catch-22 situation that neither enhances task accomplishment nor facilitates group development.

STRATEGIES FOR A GROUP LEADER TO COPE WITH PROBLEM BEHAVIORS

The strategies to combat problem behaviors proposed in Table 7.2 fall in the general categories of reflecting, blocking, confronting, ignoring, and holding individual conferences. The basic strategies for problem behaviors are the same as those described in Chapters 9 and 10 on verbal communication skills and leadership skills. It is also important to remember that the group's stage (described in Chapter 6) plays a critical role in deciding which strategy to use. For example, it is not wise for a leader to use confrontation in the group's beginning stage, as the relationship between the leader and members has not been established to the extent that members trust the leader to take care of them. Hence, confronting may do more harm than good and create discomfort among other group members. The more active interventions such as confronting or interrupting should generally be used after stage 2 is achieved and, while the more passive interventions such as reflecting and ignoring can be used in all stages, they are particularly useful in stage 1 as they tend to be non-threatening to group members.

Table 7.2 presents strategies the group leader can use in the group to reduce or eliminate problem behaviors. It is important to initiate most of the strategies in the group setting, where all members can see and participate, because the problem behaviors affect the group. Other group members also need to know what the leader is doing about the situation. Occasionally it is more suitable for the leader to talk with the offending member individually, even though the behavior is affecting the group.

Reflection

Reflection is a skill that holds a mirror up to a person about what he or she said (content), what he or she meant (meaning), and how he or she feels (emotions). It sounds as if it would be simple to reflect a verbal communication, but it is really very complex and has to be learned. People feel understood when they are accurately reflected and that is one reason why it is an effective intervention for problem behaviors. By using reflection, a leader is

Table 7.2 Problem Behaviors and Suggested Leader Strategies

Problem Behavior/Reason	Suggested Strategies in Group
Silence	
Withdrawal	Ask directly for input; encourage
Revenge	Ignore
Communication problems	Patience; reflect what they say; state how you perceive them; encourage
Personal problems	Ignore; hold individual conferences
Monopolizing	
Desire for attention	Block storytelling
Need to communicate details	Interrupt storytelling with reflection
Dislike silence	Ask them to take a moment to think about what is being experienced
Hostility	
Revenge	Reflect; self-disclose feelings; confront
Defense	Self-disclose feelings; confront
Deflect attention	Ignore and focus on the target
Rescuing	
Safety needs	Ignore; attend to safety need
Self-esteem needs	Give moderate support; block
Socializing	
Resistance to task	Confront
Self-esteem needs	Block; confront
Confusion	Patience; block
Poor Performance	
Personal problems	Hold individual conferences
Poor instructions	Provide needed information
Feelings of exclusion	Bring to group's attention
Lack of ability	Use existing strengths and other members to compensate
Irresponsible Behavior	
Immaturity	Confront; be patient
Personal problems	Hold individual conferences
Poor communication among members	Bring to group's attention and facilitate communication

(Continued)

Table 7.2 (*Continued*)

Problem Behavior/Reason	Suggested Strategies in Group
Inattentiveness	
Personal problems	Hold individual conferences
Environment	Fix
Hostility	Confront
Harassment	
Ignorance of policies	Block, inform, and report to instructor
Power and control needs	Block and report to instructor
	Block and report to instructor
Aggressiveness	
Power and control needs	Block
Hostility	Block and confront

neither agreeing with the behavior nor judging the person, just making sure he or she understands a perspective. Sometimes group members do not realize how they are coming across to others, or that their speech is confusing; reflecting back what such individuals did and said promotes self-awareness and helps clear up any misunderstandings.

For example, if a member becomes hostile and the leader believes the hostility has revenge as a goal, the leader could try to defuse some of the hostility by reflecting what the person says or does, *without labeling the behavior or person as hostile*. Sometimes a person becomes sullen and withdraws to exhibit hostility, getting revenge by not participating or by having to be drawn out. The leader could reflect this by saying something like, "Sam, you seem to have decided not to participate and your body and face are radiating anger. If you are angry with someone or the group, let's try and work it out so that you will want to join us" (both reflection and an invitation).

The important points to remember about reflection are that it:

- Simply feeds back to the individual a summary of his or her speech and actions
- Is not an interpretation
- Does not include an analysis of motive(s)
- Does not carry blame or criticism
- Does not label the person in any way

It is also important that the person doing the reflection not include personal opinions or perceptions. Those have a place in confrontation and self-disclosure, but not in reflecting. Reflecting is presented in more detail in Chapter 9.

Blocking

Blocking is a technique for refocusing someone when what he or she is doing or saying is not productive for the group or its task, and he or she needs to be redirected. This redirection should be done in a way that does not embarrass, humiliate, alienate, or anger the person, making blocking a tricky thing to pull off successfully. However, if the person is not blocked, other members become frustrated and little or no work is done on the task.

There are two parts to blocking: halting what is being done and/or said, and refocusing or redirecting. Halting what is being done or said involves some skill; a leader does not want to ignore the person by simply changing the subject, thereby making him or her feel devalued and not respected. You also do not want to label a person as boring or monopolizing, or imply that he or she is holding back the group's progress. One strategy for blocking is to quietly interrupt and apologize for doing so: "Sam, excuse me for interrupting you." Sam will generally stop talking at this point and the leader can then redirect the topic. Other ways to gently interrupt include, "I really do not like breaking in on what you are saying," "I feel I need to stop you at this point," and "You are expressing something important to you and I hope we can get back to it." The idea is to stop the other person in a way that conveys that he or she is respected and valued.

The second part of blocking is refocusing or redirecting, and is best done immediately after halting. For example, after apologizing for interrupting Sam, the leader can then go on to say that he or she would like to refocus the discussion. Let's say that Sam was complaining about availability of parking and had done so every session for several sessions. This time he was going into detail about his search and how he felt about it. One could block him by saying "Sam, excuse me for interrupting you. I realize how aggravating parking is for you and the rest of us and we can sympathize with what you are saying about it. But I would like to shift the attention from parking to an update on progress of each of us on the task." This approach halts what Sam is saying, validates his feelings about it, acknowledges similarities between members, and then redirects the topic.

Confronting

The most important point to remember about confrontation is that it is an invitation to the other person to examine his or her behavior and its impact on others. Confrontation is neither a demand nor an attack. The person must be left in a position to choose to reflect on his or her behavior and its consequences. Demands that the other person change, or attacks to help them see the "error of their ways" are not likely to be effective and will have long term negative consequences for the person and the group.

Confrontation should only be used after the relationship is established and when there is a genuine desire to continue the relationship. Confrontation can help a person to become aware of his or her actions and their impact on another person, but its benefits are not only for the person being confronted. It also helps other group members.

Problem behaviors where confronting as an intervention strategy can be helpful are:

- Socializing
- Lack of responsible behavior
- Inattentiveness
- Aggressiveness

It is very important to proceed with confronting tentatively so that it can be stopped at any point. For example, if the person being confronted becomes very upset, it is counterproductive to continue. Confrontation should also not be attacking, telling the person off, blaming, or criticizing. This means that the confronter needs to be aware of his or her personal motives for confronting and should not seek to satisfy personal needs at the other's expense. It should also be remembered that the person being confronted does not have to change because someone else wants him or her to change. The "confrontee" should be allowed enough freedom to make that choice, not have it forced on him or her.

Ignoring

One effective way of modifying behavior is to ignore the behavior one wants to eliminate or reduce and reinforce the behavior one wants to continue. Many problem behaviors should be ignored during the first few sessions as they are not yet problems for the group, nor are the reasons for the behaviors known. It is much more effective to target intervention strategies based on the rationale for the behavior rather than using a broad-brush approach. If a leader does not know the reason for a particular problem behavior, his or her intervention is likely to do more harm than good.

Ignoring means that one is aware of what the person is doing but consciously chooses not to respond to it. Ignoring is not to be confused with denial, in which there is no conscious acknowledgment of the behavior, only an unconscious awareness that allows no response because of personal issues.

Holding Individual Conferences

The previous techniques may not always be appropriate. It is usually more considerate and sensitive to speak with someone privately when there is the possibility of illness, personal problems, or crises that are causing problem behaviors. Together, the leader and group member can decide what or how much to disclose to group members.

STRATEGIES THE INSTRUCTOR CAN USE
TO COPE WITH PROBLEM BEHAVIORS

The presentation so far has focused on the group leader because that is the person who will be present in the group and implement interventions as needed, sometimes immediately. Other times, however, consultation with or observation by the instructor can help avoid problems or prevent them from escalating.

Instructor strategies are: instructing group leaders, prevention, and conferences. The primary instructor strategy is to teach the group leader reflecting and confronting skills. Associated with teaching them is encouraging and supporting the group leader to use these skills, as they are the two strategies that will be used most often with problem behaviors (see Table 7.2).

The instructor can also help prevent some problem behaviors by clearly spelling out expectations of students on the syllabus. The importance of a well-developed syllabus cannot be overestimated. Most students are inclined to follow guidelines presented in a syllabus; these guidelines can serve as a reminder when behavior starts to be a problem, and can form the basis for an instructor's action, such as removing a member from a group. The syllabus can also be a reference when an instructor discusses an individual's behavior with him or her. How to prepare a detailed syllabus is presented in Chapter 3.

Individual conferences with students are another effective strategy that is the instructor's responsibility. This strategy is usually implemented for unacceptable behavior, such as threats, harassment, or verbal abuse. The student engaging in such behavior needs to know that the instructor is aware of it, and that it will not be tolerated. When these behaviors occur an instructor is well advised to move swiftly and decisively to curb them.

Individual conferences may also be needed to ferret out what personal problems or crises are causing problem behavior. The goal is not to solve or fix the problem, but to understand it. The instructor's response is very different from that where behavior, e.g., verbal abuse, is the problem. Some guidelines for holding individual conferences follow.

- Set the tone for the meeting.
- Be prepared for the meeting.

- Focus on observable behavior.
- Carefully present the problem.
- Clarify what is meant.
- Remember the power differential.
- Expect attacks.
- Specify needed changes in behavior.

Guidelines for Individual Conferences

Set the Tone for the Meeting
The first thing to remember is that an individual conference with the student puts him or her "on the hot seat." Only if an instructor routinely has individual conferences with each student in the class will such a meeting not be viewed as being "called on the carpet." Thus, the meeting may begin with the student being scared, defensive, resentful, or angry. Indeed, some may come to the meeting with all of these feelings. This is why it is important for the instructor to proceed with tact and tentativeness. Try to make the student comfortable so that the conversation can occur.

To set the tone for the meeting that will reduce fright, defensiveness, and anger, an instructor can begin by welcoming the student. Smiling and saying hello is polite and conveys that you are observing social conventions for visitors. Frowning and not greeting the person conveys the opposite impression.

Be cordial and ask the student to be seated. Begin by stating what the concern is and then listen to the response. The best tone for a meeting of this sort is for the instructor to do more listening than talking.

Be Prepared for the Meeting
An instructor should also be prepared for the meeting. Review any work submitted to date so that you can be familiar with that particular student's performance. If university or college policy is a concern, have the relevant policies and penalties marked and readily available. Always have the syllabus, course catalogue, and student handbook available, as they can be useful.

Focus on Observable Behavior
Focus on the student's behavior, not the possible motives or attitudes. It can be very frustrating for a student to be told that he or she does not have the right attitude or that he or she needs to change an attitude. Attitudes are internal states and can only be inferred from behavior; these inferences are influenced by our personal perceptions and thus can be wrong. It is considerably more helpful to tell a student specifically which actions are of concern. Behavior is more easily changed than are attitudes.

Carefully Present the Problem
Although the behavior is a problem and the purpose of the conference is to effect a positive change, do not present the behavior in a blaming way. If an

instructor comes across as blaming and critical from the beginning, given the already intense emotional state that the student is likely to be in, the instructor is almost ensuring that the student will not listen accurately and will become defensive. The instructor must remember that he or she is an authority figure. Blaming or criticizing is apt to trigger defiance. Instead, try to be factual, unemotional, and matter-of-fact in recounting student behavior. Do not ascribe motives, but try to be receptive to a student's explanation.

Clarify What Is Meant
Listen to a student's response. The explanation may be another view of what is happening, may give additional information, or may change your perspective. To listen effectively, maintain eye contact, screen out distractions, use a slight forward lean, do not interrupt, and try not to formulate your response or next comment in advance. In other words, be open and truly listen.

The instructor should also try to understand both what a student says and his or her associated feelings. Therefore, try to use reflecting skills to make sure that what you heard was what the student meant to say. Sometimes what is heard is not what was said, or what was said was not what was meant. If the conversation continues with either of these errors, both parties will be on the wrong track and considerable misunderstanding can occur.

The feeling part of the message should be a primary focus. The content of the message is not nearly as important as the feelings; an instructor will make a mistake to screen out feelings. Even if intense emotions make one uncomfortable, one should try to gauge their intensity and identify them. One does not have to verbally respond to the feeling, but should use the information to judge what response to make and how to make it.

Listening and responding skills are presented further in Chapter 9.

Remember the Power Differential
Remember the differential in power. An instructor has considerable power over a student; students keenly feel this even if instructors do not. Instructors determine their grades, which, in turn, can have a significant impact on other parts of their lives. Instructors, myself included, would like to have students who are primarily interested in knowledge and for whom the grade is secondary. However, the reality is that such students are in the minority and while most students want knowledge, this desire is often less than the desire for a good grade. The power differential is a primary reason for being tentative in an individual conference and for carefully choosing words.

Expect Attacks
Some students may mount an offensive during the conference. They blame and criticize the instructor for their shortcomings, saying or implying that if he or she were competent, they would not have this problem. After all, a good defense is often to mount an offense. Do not become defensive or angry.

Stay focused on their behavior. There may indeed be something that needs fixing; one can note this for the next class. However, the conference is about the student's behavior and its impact on the group. Do not succumb to attempts to make you feel guilty for not being perfect or meeting everyone's needs. If you find yourself explaining why you did or did not do something, you are being defensive. If you find yourself irritated or annoyed, you are becoming angry. Avoid both states.

Specify Needed Changes in Behavior
Be specific about what changes in behavior the student must make. For example, it does not help a student to be told to be "less aggressive." He or she may not know what behavior is considered aggressive, as this can be a personal perception and can change depending on circumstances. It would be much more helpful to tell the student that he or she would be more effective and less offensive by listening to what others say, or not interrupting, or not making disparaging remarks about ideas others express, or not telling others where to sit or what to think, or speaking more slowly and softly, and so on.

Have them note and change the behaviors that are causing problems. Try to frame the needed changes in a way that permits the student some latitude regardless of policy. By doing so, an instructor gives the student some control, which may be very important. It also presents the student with an opportunity to be positive instead of feeling trounced. Use phrases like "be more effective," "perceive positively," "make a significant contribution," or "use your abilities and expertise" to frame the needed change. It can also be important to point out how the change in behavior is what is expected in the "real world." The student may need to be reminded that this classroom group experience is training and preparation for the workplace.

Have close at hand the class syllabus, catalogue, and student handbook as references. You may need to point out specific expectations of students presented in the syllabus, and/or specific policies in the catalogue or student handbook. It is a mystery why many students do not read these important documents or refer to them, but they do not. As their instructor you have a responsibility to inform them of university policies relevant to the situation, and these reference documents can strengthen your position. In some instances students need to know what the penalties are if they continue certain behaviors, such as harassment.

CHAPTER 8

Group-Level Problems and Solutions

The previous chapter addressed problem behaviors of individual group members; this chapter presents some common group-level problems, in which the group as a whole seems to engage in these behaviors; if the leader were to focus only on one member or a subgroup of members the basic root issue would not be addressed. Common group-level problems, discussed in the first half of this chapter, are:

- Anxiety
- Boredom
- Hostility
- Indirect attacks on the leader
- Withdrawal
- Silence
- Irritability
- Distractibility
- Depression

Suggested interventions will also be discussed in the second half of the chapter.

COMMON GROUP-LEVEL PROBLEMS

Anxiety

The following scenario illustrates how anxiety can emerge in a group.

> The first two sessions for a group go very well. Members seem willing to work and cooperate with reviewing the group goals and defining the tasks needed to complete the project. The third meeting begins with complaints

from several members that they are confused and frustrated, do not know what is expected of them, and need more structure. Even the members who are not voicing these complaints are nodding their heads. The leader tries at first to respond to each complaint. For example, when a member complains that he does not understand what is expected of him, the leader tries to review the requirements for the project and how the task has been divided. Another member then responds that she knows all that but still cannot get a handle on what she is supposed to do. After a while the leader stops trying to answer each person. The tension level in the group escalates significantly.

This is an example of the group expressing anxiety, not just one or two members. What they do not, or cannot, voice is that they are anxious, fearful, and in need of reassurance. The leader, like most leaders and instructors, is trying to answer with content, when the most important part of the message is the feelings.

What makes the problem most likely to be anxiety and not a real need for structure or information? The group's stage in its life span is the answer. The group is in the first stage, when anxiety manifested in questioning behavior, calls for more information and structure, and expressions of confusion and frustration are common. What members are really seeking is evidence that the leader is competent and can and will take care of them; that it is safe in the group; and that they will have what they need to get the job done. The leader and instructor have most likely provided enough factual information about the task, the group, and expectations for students, so lack of information is not the real issue. Of course, if there are gaps in needed information, they should be filled. However, even when that situation exists, providing more information will not address the basic concern—that is, anxiety.

Boredom

Boredom can be openly expressed, indirectly expressed, or not expressed at all. An illustration of open expression of boredom follows.

The group has had five sessions. In the sixth session, after a couple of members have given an update on their progress on the project, a member looks at the leader and says that she is bored. Another member chimes in and says that he feels the session is not productive, and others start making comments about being stuck. Even the members who have made reports this session comment that they had a hard time thinking of something to say. The leader is at a loss for how to address the complaints. Members go on to say that they are tired of meetings, do not think the group is worthwhile, and wonder how they are expected to learn anything if this keeps up. As they talk, the leader becomes more and more discouraged.

At this point, many leaders will ask members what can be done to change things so that they are not bored. What leaders are overlooking, however, is that members are using the concept of boredom to express concern about something that is being suppressed in the group. It may not be unusual for one or two members to be distracted and uninterested during a session, as personal concerns can cause this to happen, but it is unusual for many, most, or all group members to feel this way at the same time. The group leader needs to think about what the real message is.

One possible and not at all unusual message is that there is unexpressed conflict in the group. Members are terming the group "boring" because they are suppressing some important feelings, usually negative ones. They may not know how to, or do not feel comfortable expressing these feelings, so they turn them on the group. If the group leader fails to recognize that this is the real message, members will continue to feel this way and the group will get bogged down.

Hostility

The following scenario exhibits typical group hostility in action.

> The seventh session starts off with one member asking the leader why they are being asked to meet so often. When the leader points out that it is a class requirement, members groan and start complaining that they do not need so many meetings. As the leader tries to change the topic to one that addresses the assigned project, members begin to challenge the direction of the group. The leader is told that he seems indifferent to what the group wants and needs, that he does not structure the task appropriately, and that the group is not on track. The members say in direct and indirect ways that the leader is to blame for how they feel and what they perceive to be the lack of progress and productivity of the group.

When something like this happens the group leader can easily feel defensive, attacked, overwhelmed, and unfairly treated. It takes some thought and experience to realize that although one is indeed being attacked and treated unfairly, this is normal for the group and to be expected. The group is in stage 2 of its development and attacks on the leader are characteristic of this stage. The leader must accept that this is what groups do, and not take the remarks personally or become defensive.

It is very easy to identify when the group is hostile apart from attacks on the leader. Members seem willing to go to battle over the least little thing. Namecalling, labeling, impatience, and angry expressions become common. This behavior is uncommon in classroom groups; it is presented here only because some unfortunate soul may encounter this situation. The group leader and the instructor need to know that this is a very destructive situation and that drastic measures are needed. Without trying to identify the causes for the sustained hostility, the group should be disbanded. Find some other way for the students to complete the project. This is one problem that will be beyond leaders' and instructors' expertise and time constraints to solve.

Indirect Attacks on the Leader

Open and direct hostility is most easily identified when the group is venting and making sure the leader knows of its displeasure. However, indirect hostility is another form of group attack, and because it is indirect it is often overlooked or discounted. It is no less important for often going unrecognized Indirect attacks affect the group's progress because until this form of hostility is resolved the group does not continue to develop and move into stage 3, where cohesiveness and productivity are increased.

How can a leader identify an indirect attack? First, the group has successfully completed stage 1; that is, the group has met for more than roughly two or three sessions.

The second clue comes from the internal emotional experience of the group leader. Even though the group is now a relatively familiar and comfortable place, the leader may realize during or after a meeting that he or she feels churned up inside and is not sure why. No one person in the group did or said anything to produce the feelings, but somehow, the leader feels "pelted" by the group with something.

The third clue comes from listening carefully to what is said and meant. When one listens carefully one can better understand what the speaker means and pick up the real message. If, when one is listening, one senses that no matter what their words and the manner, the speakers are critical, then that is probably the actual message.

The following is an example of a probable indirect attack on the leader.

A group is in the fifth session and for some unknown reason the discussion turns to decisions made early in the group. Several decisions are revisited, and when they get to the one on how the leader would be chosen, some members voice the wish that they had made some other decision. Instead of electing one leader, they now think they would have liked to have a rotating leader. They quickly voice that they have nothing against the current leader, but wish they had better understood their choices. The leader is confused by the group's discussion that revisits previous decisions and by comments that express a desire for a different kind of leadership accompanied by protests that they do not mean anything negative about him. This is most likely a disguised indirect attack on the leader.

Withdrawal

An example to illustrate withdrawal follows:

> The group has met weekly for eight sessions. During the previous session, a conflict between two members erupted and expanded to include other members. The contention was that some minority members felt that other members were treating them with a lack of respect. The leader was able to diffuse the emotional intensity and assist members in working through the conflict. It is now the middle of the eighth session, and all members are uncharacteristically silent and withdrawn. Most will not initiate discussion or volunteer their input, although all respond readily enough when asked. The leader feels that the group is bogged down and trying to get anything done is very difficult.

What has happened could have been anticipated by the group leader. Almost every time there is an emotionally intense session, the next one is quiet and members are withdrawn. Members may fear that the issue is not resolved and that the same level of emotional intensity will surface, and feel reluctant to get that involved again.

Another reason may be that the issue is not resolved; the conflict is smoldering and members are trying hard not to let it erupt again. They are making an effort to suppress their real feelings, and this suppression is manifested through the silence and withdrawal.

There are other, related reasons why groups may be withdrawn for a session when they usually actively participate. These reasons are usually associated with suppression of important feelings, whether positive or negative. Several, or all, group members may be suppressing feelings, and they have to limit their engagement by reducing participation.

Silence

Just as the silent member's behavior is troubling to the group, so is a group-level silence. An illustration follows.

> This group has always been somewhat silent. Most members say that they are quiet and like to take time to think before they speak. The leader has accommodated this characteristic and does not expect lively exchanges.
>
> However, it is the sixth session and the quiet group is quieter than usual. Even when the leader asks directly for input members reply with only one word or a shrug. The leader tells the group that they seem quieter than usual but no one responds.

This scenario points out the differences in silence. It is very difficult to describe silences so that differences can be understood. However, anyone who has experienced various silences can attest to their distinct differences. In this instance the leader is aware of a difference because this week's silence has a very different quality and intensity than the customary one.

Most likely, members are suppressing conflict with the leader. They want to attack but may not feel safe to do so, are unsure they would be supported by other members, dislike the leader and so do not want to disagree or be in conflict, or do not want to disturb the harmony in the group. Whatever the reason(s), the group would rather be silent than speak out.

Irritability

Groups, like individuals, get cranky and irritable. An example follows.

> The ninth of fourteen sessions seems characterized by restlessness and irritability. Topics are changed with no warning or for no apparent reason; members fidget in their seats; some get up and move around, then sit down only to jump up again; others seem to snap at and take issue with whatever is said. The group is out of sorts. The leader tries several times to focus the discussions but has little success. Nothing works to improve the mood or atmosphere, and finally, the leader gives up. Everyone leaves dissatisfied with the group and its progress.

This group is likely becoming aware that it will end. There is an unspoken panic around termination and all that implies, which is exhibited in "grumping." Even if the task is proceeding on time, it does not seem to make a difference, as members become aware on a nonconscious level that the time for the group's ending is drawing near. If this state continues unrecognized for upcoming sessions, group meetings will remain very uncomfortable.

The panic is around events, task completion, and ending the group. Task completion is at the forefront because the task is the major grade determinant. Ending the group is on a more personal, affective level, for relationships will be forever ended or changed. While there will be some relief that they no longer have to attend group sessions, there will also be some sadness at ending sources of support, encouragement, and interpersonal learning. If the group has attended to developing relationships and providing support and encouragement, then members cannot help but feel a void when this is taken away. None of this is meant to imply that members will be devastated because the group is ending. The sadness will be mild unless very strong relationships have developed. Nonetheless, even mild sadness affects people, especially unacknowledged or unsensed sadness. Hence, the restlessness and general irritation. The group will continue to deal with termination issues until the group ends. The aware leader can do much to facilitate the process and keep the group from premature termination.

Distractibility

Members and the group as a whole can become distracted. An illustration follows.

> The seventh session begins with members laughing, joking, and chatting with each other. Everyone seems in a good mood and the leader is encouraged to think that this is going to be a good session. She starts by summarizing what has been accomplished and what still needs to be done. As she is talking, two members are having a quiet conversation, some are looking at the floor, and one other member has pushed his chair back out of the circle and sits slumped. Two other members arrive late, laughing as they enter the room, and begin to tell the group a funny story about another class. Other members chime in and begin to relate their stories and anecdotes with much laughter. The leader sits and wonders what happened and what is going on with the group.

The group has become distracted from both their cognitive and their affective tasks. When groups become distracted it can take many forms, such as increased storytelling, socializing, talking about abstract or intellectual topics not a part of the group's mission, such as politics, and physical restlessness. Since the group has been meeting for some time, the distractibility is not due to anxiety and unfamiliarity with each other and the process. It is more likely due to a discomfort about decisions made, extent of goal accomplishment, an unrecognized problem in the group, or an unwillingness to address concerns openly. Any or all of these may be why the group is unable to focus its energy.

Even an experienced group leader may not be sure what the real reason for the group's behavior is, but is more likely to understand that it is one or more of the above reasons. The novice group leader will become frustrated and may even resort to blaming, chastising, and giving orders; none of which will address the problem or produce a solution. What the leader needs to understand is that the group is doing this for a reason, not just to be contrary.

Depression

This group-level problem is included here because it is not addressed in most books that deal with group work, with the possible exception of books on group psychotherapy. However, the depressed group is found not only in therapy groups but also in many work groups, although it tends to be unrecognized. The following discussion is intended to help the instructor and group leader realize when they may be dealing with a depressed group.

Why even discuss this topic, since making the diagnosis and providing treatment are very likely outside the expertise of the target audience for this book? It is important because it may help the instructor and others involved to better understand their feelings and to avoid frustration when little or nothing works to make the experience pleasant or better.

In their book *Mind/Body Health,* Hafen and colleagues (1996) estimate that "about 7 percent of all women and 3 percent of all men have major depression; another 4–5 percent have minor depression and 8 percent have major anxiety disorders" (216). They go on to point out that the percentage of teenagers with diagnosed clinical depression has increased more than fivefold over the past 40 years. If these estimates are applied to a college class of 20 women and 10 men, the instructor could expect that 2 to 3 students would have major depression, another 1 to 2 would have minor depression, and another 2 to 3 would have major anxiety disorders. This is quite a few students who are depressed and/or anxious to the point where it significantly affects their mood. Add to this the description by Richard Sword of the depression-prone personality (Hafen et al., 1996) which says that this person is "ambitious, conscientious, responsible, and hard-working; has a high standard of personal honesty and integrity; is generally pleasant and seems to be happy, even when inwardly sad, and rarely shows anger." p. 221. The result is that almost all instructors can expect to have a few students who are suffering from depression and/or anxiety.

The effect of a depressed person on a group is significant and, when there are two or more such students, it can be disastrous if not recognized and carefully handled. "Carefully handled" does not mean that therapy should be attempted, but that the situation needs to be dealt with for the benefit of all group members. What generally happens is that both the instructor and the group leader sense that there is something awry and try several interventions, none of which will have a significant impact. Other members who are not depressed or anxious nonetheless seem to absorb the attitudes of hopelessness, frustration, sadness, and dissatisfaction and act on them, making the group a despairing one.

Most of the time group members seem able to work around these attitudes; even though they may not enjoy the group work, they are able to be productive. However, there are times when several depressives end up in the same group and that is a situation ripe for disaster. The members, the leader, and the instructor all try hard to identify problems and work them out. They give considerable energy to working in the group and on relationships, but nothing seems to make a difference. The group is still bogged down and unpleasant to be in. The harder everyone tries, the worse everything gets. This is extremely frustrating for all concerned.

Depending on the severity of the depression in the group, the instructor may need to consider disbanding the group and having members work in dyads or triads. Group work under these conditions is counterproductive; only someone who understands the etiology, course of development, and treatment for depression would be able to effectively handle the group. Since most instructors want to use the group to teach content, even experienced therapists or those who teach therapy would find that it takes too much effort to continue the group and that learning content would suffer.

RESPONSE AND INTERVENTION STRATEGIES FOR GROUP-LEVEL PROBLEMS

General Guidelines

Leaders will need to respond on two levels to group problems: personally, by looking within; and externally, by applying specific intervention strategies in the group. Table 8.1 addresses the former, and Table 8.2 the latter. The responses and interventions in these tables were developed with the assumptions that both the instructor and the student group leader were unfamiliar with group work or had limited experience, and that what was needed could be easily implemented. It is important to remember that each problem can have several causes and that no one strategy is effective for every problem. Further, making an error in diagnosing the problem or choosing an effective strategy is not a fatal mistake. The group will likely not be harmed; it will probably just continue to exhibit the problem behavior, and both the leader and members will be increasingly frustrated. Consequently, there is considerable room for trying various strategies. Further, the group itself will also play a part; groups differ in their personalities and reactions, making the choice of an effective intervention more complex.

Whatever intervention is used should be implemented with the emotional state of members as the primary concern. After all, their emotional state plays an important part in task accomplishment, group productivity, and achievement of one of the class goals: learning to work in teams or work cooperatively.

The other point to keep in mind, especially for the student group leader, is not to take what the group says or does as a personal attack or criticism, even if they mean it to be one. At that point, the basic problem is not yours, you are just the focus for their concerns. You will be considerably more effective if you can resist acting on feelings of being criticized, blamed, or put down. It is also important to use both the verbal and nonverbal communication skills, as those are basic for all interventions and will be particularly helpful for group-level intervention strategies.

Anxiety

On a personal level, one of the most helpful things group leaders can learn is how to manage their own anxiety. Even the most experienced and capable

Table 8.1 Group-Level Problems and Helpful Leader Personal Responses

Problem	Helpful Personal Responses
Anxiety	Contain and manage personal anxiety
	Acknowledge feeling anxious to members
Boredom	Increase effort to be present-centered
	Silently explore reason for boredom
Hostility to leader	Do not become defensive
	Do not attack
	Do not take it personally
Hostility among members	Do not ignore or avoid
Indirect attacks on the leader	Do not apologize or overexplain
	Recognize it as an attack
	*See Hostility to leader, above
Withdrawal	Stay in touch with what is happening in the group
	Reflect on events prior to the withdrawal
Silence	Contain and manage personal anxiety
	Do not end session early
Irritability	Do not criticize or chastise group
	Contain and manage personal anxiety
Distractibility	Do not become irritated
Depression	Do not "catch" depressed feelings

group leaders cannot eliminate feeling anxious in the group, but what sets them apart and increases their effectiveness is their ability to identify, contain, and manage their anxiety.

Managing anxiety allows one to model that anxiety is not to be feared, repressed, or denied and that it is possible to function effectively in spite of feeling anxious. It is surprising just how many people do not realize this. They spend enormous amounts of time and energy trying not to feel anxious, which leads to their feeling even more anxious or, if they do succeed in repressing it, the anxiety may express itself in less desirable ways, such as physical health problems.

The first step in managing personal anxiety is to identify and acknowledge it to oneself. One should feel where the tension is located and how it is manifested in physical sensations—tight stomach or shoulder muscles, clenched teeth, upset stomach, sweating, and so on. After identifying and accepting the anxiety, do not try to make it go away. Do not try to distract or talk yourself out of feeling anxious. It is more effective to accept that you are

Table 8.2 Group-Level Problems and Associated Intervention Strategies

Problem	Strategies
Anxiety	Open discussion about feeling anxious
	Reflect feelings as well as content
	Summarize group accomplishments
Boredom	Use an energizing activity
	Use an exercise on feelings or conflict
	Ask members to be present-centered
Hostility to leader	Reflect what was said
	Defuse intensity
Hostility among members	Use conflict resolution strategies
	Block namecalling, verbal abuse
	Consult with instructor
Indirect attacks on the leader	Use active listening
	Reflect both content and feelings
Withdrawal	Use tension-reliever exercise
	Focus on content, cognitive tasks
	Use exercise on conflict
	Use exercise on feelings
Silence	Use nonverbal exercise
	Make a provocative statement
	Summarize group accomplishments
Irritability	Introduce termination
	Review goals and timeline
Distractibility—early	Focus on unexpressed anxiety
Distractibility—later	Review goals and timeline
	Discuss future directions
Depression	Consult with instructor

anxious but use affirming self-talk to remember that it can be contained and controlled; it need not overwhelm. The final step in managing anxiety is to cognitively think about how to proceed and not act or react based on feelings. Consciously decide what is the best action for oneself and the group.

One way a leader can help members manage group-level anxiety is to admit openly to having similar feelings. This will give members permission to acknowledge their anxiety. I always acknowledge my anxiety and tension when I begin a group. I do not go into a lot of detail, but make a short simple statement about feeling nervous.

This opens the door for a more open discussion of members' anxiety. The usual result is that anxiety is reduced, not increased. During discussion, the leader can reflect not just the content but also the feelings expressed to help members openly acknowledge their anxiety. In this way members begin to realize that they are not alone in feeling anxious and that it is helpful to openly acknowledge feelings.

If group-level anxiety occurs in the middle or later stage of the group's development the leader can use a strategy that focuses on reassuring group members that they are making satisfactory progress toward their cognitive goal: completion of the project. Summarize accomplishments to date and do not emphasize what has not yet been finished, even if the group is somewhat behind where they should be. Members know what they have and have not done; by highlighting accomplishments, the leader reduces the likelihood that members will perceive him or her as criticizing and blaming.

Boredom

Boredom generally occurs as a response to suppressing some important feelings. With boredom the energy flies to outside-group concerns, making the person uninterested in here-and-now activity in the group. He or she would rather be somewhere else, doing something else. The group has little or no appeal and seems dull and uninviting.

The group leader can ask members to become present-centered and to talk about what makes it difficult to be fully "there" in the group. Why isn't the group more interesting and appealing? Other interventions are specific exercises to analyze and alleviate the boredom.

Energizing Exercises
Most group energizing exercises involve physical movement and fun. The objectives are to get people moving and laughing. When members have to become physically active, they must bring their attention to the present. When they laugh, feelings of well-being are produced which, in turn, tend to transfer to how they feel about the group. Once attention, feelings of well-being, and better feelings about the group occur, the group becomes flooded with energy and members are no longer bored. Some energizing exercises are described in Chapter 11.

Conflict Resolution Exercises
If the expressed boredom is a result of suppressed feelings and/or expression of conflict in the group, then an exercise that focuses on conflict can help. The exercise can teach members to understand the effects of expressed and unexpressed feelings about conflicts, or can teach them other ways of behaving in conflict situations. Using an exercise gives members permission to express

conflict, which energizes the group and then allows the leader to proceed with conflict intervention strategies, such as those described in Chapter 6. Exercises to make conflict more visible or contribute to conflict resolution are in Chapter 11.

Diffusing Hostility

Hostility in the group can be very destructive if not immediately addressed. When hostility is expressed toward the leader it can be very unexpected and, for that reason, difficult to handle. When the leader is faced with group hostility, the primary point to remember in dealing with it on a personal level is to not become defensive or retaliatory. Explaining, apologizing, and pointing out how members are unfair and wrong do not help the situation or the group. It is much more productive and constructive to reflect back to the group what they have said and meant in a nonjudgmental, neutral way. It could be that some, or all, members did not fully realize that they were being hostile. They may have wanted to convey some discomfort or displeasure, but did not consciously intend to be hostile. The leader's use of reflection makes them more aware, and then dialogue can begin without hostility.

However, if the hostility toward the leader is an honest and fair expression of feelings in the group, then other interventions are needed. The instructor should attend a session as soon as possible. There is something at work in the group that needs immediate attention from the "authority," that is, the instructor.

If the entire group seems hostile to one another, then the leader needs to quickly intervene to block inappropriate verbal expressions, such as name-calling, abuse, disdain, or contempt. The leader should take care when using blocking as an intervention that one member or subgroup does not appear to be favored over another. Those engaging in the behavior should not be criticized or blamed, just stopped. Remember, this hostility has likely built up over time. The leader is probably not aware of what has contributed to it, which is one of many reasons why he or she does not want to appear to take sides. If the hostility is intense, the leader will need to consult with the instructor and/or use conflict intervention strategies (see Chapter 6).

Indirect Attacks on the Leader

Most attacks on the leader are indirect and may not appear, on the surface, to carry much effect. However, there are very likely deeper, more intense feelings connected to the attack, which indicates that it is important to the group and its development.

Recognition of indirect attacks may be difficult; they can be so subtle that the novice group leader never recognizes them. One sign of becoming more adept at being a group leader is the ability to recognize indirect attacks when they are being launched. For assistance in detecting attacks, review the expected behaviors for stage 2, described in Chapter 5.

The most effective strategies are to not become defensive and to not turn the attack back on the group. This is another instance in which the group leader has to live with anxiety. The group leader should also use the technique of reflection of what was said and the associated feelings. Sometimes, all members really want to know is that they are being heard and understood.

Withdrawal

It can be very disconcerting to have the group withdraw. The first inclination is to try to get them involved by telling them that they seem uninvolved. This seldom works. Members will then report various excuses for not being fully present in the group: they are tired, feel sick, or have personal problems. These excuses may all be true and real, but are not sufficient reasons for "fading away" from the group.

There may be very different reasons for the withdrawal, such as group tension or conflict. The leader must first try to discern the reason for the withdrawal and then select the intervention.

If the reason for "fadeaway" is tension in the group, then an exercise to relieve tension may help. If there is unexpressed conflict, an exercise on conflict and conflict resolution may help. If suppressed feelings are the source of the fadeaway, then an exercise on feelings is called for. If the group is avoiding the emotional intensity of the previous session, the leader can emphasize cognitive tasks.

Prolonged Silence

Periods of silence can be expected in a group. Sometimes members need time to reflect, and sometimes the silence is comfortable and companionable. However, prolonged silence usually means there is something awry in the group. The quality of this kind of silence is different; there is an underlying tension that is very uncomfortable.

With this silence, the leader needs to be able to contain his or her personal anxiety and not rush to fill the space with something trivial. Further, if interventions do not work, the leader must resist the inclination to end the session early. It may appear that nothing is happening or that group members do not want to cooperate or participate, but there is something important going on in the group that needs immediate attention.

Active intervention strategies include using a nonverbal communication exercise, reviewing goals and progress to date, with an emphasis on accomplishments, or tossing out provocative statements as a surprise. Prolonged silence provides an opportunity to do something innovative and unexpected.

Irritability

Sustained irritability in a session usually accompanies unexpressed or unconscious anxiety about termination of the group. The most useful strategy is for the leader to introduce the idea of termination by noting how much time the group has left to work and soliciting ideas for how to best accomplish the task and have a satisfactory ending to the group. Emphasis should be on task accomplishment and relationships. While there can be some relief that they do not have to attend meetings, members will also feel some sadness about leaving the relationship that has developed.

Distractibility

When many group members become distracted in the early stages of group, it means something different than if it happens in the later stages. In the early stages, distraction usually indicates anxiety, and the most helpful intervention is to address the anxiety (see the discussions on anxiety earlier in this chapter).

When members are distracted in the later stages of group, it usually means that there is some unexpressed concern or dissatisfaction with their performance or progress. The leader can remain patient and introduce a goal checkup, a review of the timeline, and a discussion of future directions for the group. This gives the members an opening to express any discontent in a direct way that can be addressed more constructively. If the leader does not know their complaints or source of dissatisfaction, then he or she cannot make adjustments that could be helpful.

Depression

As noted earlier in this chapter, the only helpful intervention with a depressed group is to consult with the instructor and seriously consider disbanding the group. There is more than one way to accomplish the learning for the class; continuing to try to make the group and the leader work under these conditions is counterproductive.

CHAPTER 9

Relating Characteristics and Communication Skills

Relating, communication, and group leadership skills and characteristics are needed to have an effective and productive group. Skills, the focus of this and the next chapter, are specific behaviors and activities that can be learned or enhanced. Characteristics are personal inner states that are an inherent part of the individual; they cannot be directly taught but can be developed through personal growth. Certain nonverbal behaviors indicate the presence or absence of the feelings and attitudes that constitute characteristics.

Relating characteristics foster the development, maintenance, and strengthening of relationships (Verderber & Verderber, 1992). Developing positive relationships is the single most important step in conducting and participating in a productive group. Relating characteristics exhibited by the group leader provide members with assurance of safety, faith that trust can be given and received, confidence that each member will be treated as a valued individual, and surety that the task will be accomplished. Commitment to the group and its task results from use of positive relating skills. The characteristics in this category are attending, acceptance, warmth and caring, genuineness, tolerance, and being nonjudgmental.

Communication skills are also crucial in developing the group and fostering its growth and task accomplishment (Carroll et al., 1997; Corey & Corey, 1998). Communication is both verbal and nonverbal, with the nonverbal component often carrying the primary part of the message. Since many nonverbal gestures and behaviors define existing relationships, these are considered relating characteristics. This discussion on communication skills focuses on verbal communication. The skills presented are paraphrasing, reflection, reframing, clarifying, summarizing, confronting, giving constructive feedback, immediacy, and concreteness.

The group leadership skills discussed in Chapter 10 are those that complement the skills discussed in this chapter and are especially effective when used in a group. All these skills, in conjunction with relating and communicating characteristics, form a set of competencies that enable the leader to develop a productive, effective, and efficient group.

RELATING CHARACTERISTICS

Relationships are built over time and do not instantly form. They take time and effort to maintain and all parties must contribute if the relationship is to be meaningful and grow. These are only two of many reasons why the group leader needs to be patient and to take steps to develop positive relationships with and among group members. Positive relationships in the group foster productivity, commitment, a sense of community, and a feeling of pride and confidence. Negative or inadequate relationships have opposite effects; the group is unproductive or less productive than its talents would indicate. For example, members may have little or no commitment to the group and its goals; there may be no sense of community, no shared liking and respect; and members may have little or no sense of pride and confidence about the group or its accomplishments. Clearly, developing positive relationships is a critical component for positive outcomes.

Attending

When we give others our full attention, they usually feel valued, respected, and interesting. To attend successfully, one must first decide to do so and screen out distractions. Focus on the person or group as they are, at that moment. Do not think about the past, the future, or personal concerns; focus on the present and the person(s). Once one is present-centered, one can begin to make sure one's nonverbal behavior conveys one's attending. Gestures, body posture, and facial expressions are the most accurate reflection of attention; they are the clues that others read and react to. One does not convince anyone of attending merely by saying so. Others perceive attention based on their reading of nonverbal behavior.

The nonverbal behaviors that convey attending are:

- Pleasant facial expression
- Slight forward lean
- Body oriented to person or group
- Eye contact
- Open arm position (e.g., not folded across chest)

One word of caution about attending: when it is used too intensely or with the intent to control, dominate, or intimidate, there will be negative results. The other person will become defensive, closed, and withdrawn.

Acceptance

Being open promotes acceptance of another person as valued and respected. The willingness to get to know another person before making evaluations promotes relationships. The person who appears to be closed, critical, and disapproving is not an appealing partner in a relationship.

Feeling accepted contributes to members' willingness to invest time and effort in the group, for they feel that they will be included and not excluded or rejected. This perception by members is important to developing feelings of trust and safety.

Acceptance is a skill that has to be developed; the first step is to become aware of one's preferences and values. Everyone is a product of his or her experiences, and these form our personalities and ways of perceiving and valuing. Ferreting out our preferences and values and coming to terms with them is a life long process. However, the leader of the group has an opportunity to become more consciously aware of what they are.

Steps to foster and convey acceptance include:

- Listening to all members
- Soliciting and use input from all members
- Blocking disparaging or demeaning remarks
- Blocking attacks on members who have different viewpoints or ideas
- Not taking sides in disagreements or disputes

The leader must not appear to favor one member over another. Certainly, he or she is entitled to personal preferences and viewpoint, but there are ways to make these known without alienating any member. Further, the mission and goal for the group will not be accomplished if the leader is perceived as playing favorites.

Warmth and Caring

Group members are very anxious at the beginning of group. There is considerable confusion about the task, the group, and what they are expected to do. This is not unusual but can be helped some if the leader makes them feel welcomed and confident of accomplishing the stated goals. One aspect of making members feel welcomed and included is the ability of the leader to convey warmth and caring. Members will feel excluded when they perceive the leader as cool and aloof. Under these conditions they will remain withdrawn, anxious, and wary. They will not feel that the leader cares about their welfare and, in return, they will not care about the group.

Warmth and caring are conveyed by facial expressions, body postures, tone of voice, and words chosen. Facial expressions are not always the best indication of what someone is feeling, as many have learned not to show their feelings on their face. However, the group leader can take care to have a pleasant expression on his or her face, especially at the beginning of the group or session. A pleasant expression is not a neutral one; it involves a smile and open eyes, without hands on the face. Look at others, obtain eye contact if possible, and smile. Narrowed eyes, shifting eyes, or eyes that focus on the forehead or nose do not convey warmth.

Body posture also contributes to conveying warmth and caring. One should orient his or her body toward the other(s), avoid folding arms across the chest, and have a relaxed and open body position. One gesture that some people use to convey that they are "just one of the gang" is to turn a chair around so that the back faces others and sit on it facing the group. Rather than conveying inclusion, this presents a barrier between the person and others, and is a gesture of superior status.

Tone of voice is a significant signal for warmth and caring. Take care not to talk too fast and not to clip words. Try for a voice tone that sounds inviting and that conveys happiness in making their acquaintance. Treat others as valued guests.

Select words that are specific and direct in conveying friendliness. Do not resort to asking a lot of questions, but make open statements that invite the other person to respond. At the first meeting, leaders should be sure to greet members individually, introduce themselves, and let members know that they feel in the same boat, perhaps opening the floor for discussion of "new-group jitters." What leaders say in the beginning is very important and sets the tone for members to begin feeling comfortable and a part of the group.

These are some behaviors that convey warmth and caring in the beginning of the group. As the group develops, warmth and caring are still important, but not as necessary for members to feel comfortable. A leader in the latter stages can use the same verbal and nonverbal behaviors, but can also be freer to express displeasure, discomfort, or concern.

Genuineness

The authentic person is "real" and honest, which promotes trust in others. This person can be relied on to be truthful and to allow others to see their "real" selves carried out to the ideal. It is not necessary for an effective group leader to meet this ideal; it is sufficient for that person to be as open and honest as possible so that members can trust him or her.

In some ways, genuineness is a characteristic that cannot be taught or learned. It is an integral part of a person. However, there are some behaviors that can express genuineness and facilitate relationships: not having a hidden agenda, telling the truth and giving all available information, admitting error, and being willing to express feelings.

Tolerance

Some people eagerly embrace the new, the untried, and the different. They are intrigued by novelty and willingly seek it out. They do not view differences as reasons to be cautious or rejecting. Others are more tentative and wary in their perceptions and actions, preferring to take time before jumping in or making a choice. These people tend to view differences between themselves and others as important but not necessarily something to keep them apart. Still others view differences between themselves and other people as threatening and tend to remain aloof and rejecting.

It is important for group leaders to develop tolerance for differences in others, as this is what they will most likely face in their groups and in the workplace when they begin their careers. Members will sense when the leader does not like or approve of them, and this reaction will make it impossible to build trust within the group. Further, an attitude of intolerance communicates itself to other members, and they begin to model it and become rejecting.

Tolerance, like genuineness, is partly an internal state or characteristic, and intolerance develops out of experiences and the acculturation process. Still, one can consciously develop tolerance out of a desire to be accepting of differences in others. In the maturing process, one can recognize that others are different, but not attach value judgments to them because of the differences. Tolerance is also affected by the conscious examination of values, biases, and prejudices. It can increase with awareness of some formerly unconscious assumptions, both good and bad, about the value of others and a decision to hold on or to let go of them. This is not an easy process, but it does lead to increased tolerance.

COMMUNICATION SKILLS

This discussion is focused primarily on verbal communication skills, which can be learned and refined through practice. Indeed, these skills should be practiced until they are second nature. Communication skills are helpful in building and maintaining satisfying relationships both in the workplace and in one's personal life.

Paraphrasing

Paraphrasing is not parroting. Yes, one does try to rephrase the content of what the other person said, but one has a different purpose for repeating what was said. The reasons are twofold: to understand correctly what the person said, and to affirm that what was heard was what the person meant to say. Paraphrasing distills the message's content and gives back the essence.

Paraphrasing is helpful when someone is trying to make a point that is getting lost in the details or the story. Sometimes what the speaker says does not appear to be clear or relevant or to make sense. Paraphrasing can help others see the connection or make sense of the message; it can also help the speaker clarify or change the words to more accurately reflect their intent.

To paraphrase, one needs to:

- Stop talking
- Focus on the speaker
- Not formulate responses
- Hear the content and the essential content of the message
- Report or say what was heard, not what is imagined was meant
- Not use the same words as the speaker

Reflection

Reflection occurs when one can discuss both the cognitive and the affective aspects of the message. The affective part of the message is the most important part because it tells the kind, level, and intensity of emotions associated with the content. The feeling part tells the receiver just how significant the communication is for the speaker.

Learning to tune in to feelings begins with increasing awareness of what the other person is experiencing. When one begins to try to reflect feelings, one may be inaccurate in perceptions, but practice can help increase ability to be accurate. Further, others will begin to appreciate the attempts, however inexperienced, to understand their feelings, which thereby improves the relationships.

A leader may want to first practice reflecting when the emotional content does not appear to be intense. Being incorrect at such a time is less likely to irritate the speaker than when he or she is very emotional. Further, it may seem easier to judge when someone is very emotional, but reflecting that emotion may not make the person feel understood; it is more likely to make him or her feel criticized or belittled.

Learning to observe and understand nonverbal communication can be helpful in developing ability to be accurate in reflecting. Facial expressions, body positions, and gestures are vital clues to others' feelings and are more accurate indicators of emotional content than are words used. For example, if a friend says, "I don't think you should do that," with a frown, her arms folded across her chest, and her fists clenched, it conveys a very different feeling than when she uses exactly the same words with wide eyes, sustained eye contact, her arms open at her sides, and a slight forward lean.

Reframing

Leaders will find this communication skill to be an advantage, especially when trying to mediate conflicts, or when members cannot seem to find words to express their thoughts. The task is to understand what the person means or is attempting to convey, and express it in more acceptable or understandable ways. For example, if a member says something sarcastic in trying to express frustration, the leader could reframe the comment to express the frustration. The sarcastic remark is not helpful, the reframe could be.

This skill differs from reflection in that the leader will have to guess what the member's intent is, and use his or her own words to express it. Reflecting does not add or infer anything, but reframing may. In the example above, the leader could reframe the frustration as the member's desire to do a good job but the constraints seem overwhelming at this time. These are inferences and additions.

Another advantage for this skill is that the leader gets an opportunity to turn what appears to be a negative comment into a more positive one. Making the comment positive can help moderate intense negative feelings, reduce defensiveness, and channel energy in more constructive ways.

Clarifying

To clarify means to make something clearer to the listener. There is some misunderstanding, ambiguity, confusion, etc., that is keeping others from understanding what is meant or intended. Until this is cleared up the group is stuck. Members are talking at cross purposes.

The leader too may not fully understand what the person was trying to say. In this event, the leader would begin the process of clarifying by stating what he or she thought the person said. This would be verified before proceeding to the next step which is to then report what the leader considers to be the meaning or intent. If the meaning or intent is not understood or only partially understood, this gives the member an opportunity to restate and try to better say what was intended. If the member is confused and cannot find adequate means of expression, the leader can then use a series of questions asking if this is what the member meant. The leader should pause after each question to give the member an opportunity to respond.

Clarification can be very important, especially since it is very possible that words and concepts will be used that have several meanings. For example, this weekend and next weekend can mean different times for individuals. This weekend for some means the upcoming weekend. For others it can mean the weekend that just passed. The next weekend for some may mean the upcoming weekend, while for others it is the weekend following the upcoming one. If the various meanings are not clarified everyone thinks they are talking about the same time frame when in fact, they are talking about different ones.

Summarizing

When you summarize for groups, you report on highlights for the topic, session, or progress of the group to that point. This is valuable because summarization helps keep members focused on the task and aware of relationships and what is happening. It also provides a goal checkup. It is all too easy for members and the group to become so caught up in events and activities that they lose sight of the primary task and goal for the group. Periodic summarizing is a necessary task and skill.

The leader can summarize during a session. This has the effect of highlighting present functioning. It can also be used to point out progress, lack of progress, or that a task is finished and it is time to move on.

It can be helpful to some groups if the group leader will summarize progress to date at the beginning of a session. This summary is not necessary for every session, but could be used every third or fourth session. Groups with members who are task-oriented and very concrete may benefit from this summarization. A group leader can consult the minutes in preparing for this summary.

The end of the session summary is a good means to effectively end a group. Summarizing at this point highlights accomplishments and can reinforce decisions made or tasks assigned.

Confronting

Confrontation does not mean attacking. It is supposed to be an honest and open expression of your perspective and an invitation to the other person to present his or her perspective. You seem to have differences of perspective and want to work them out (Daniels and Horowitz, 1984; Johnson and Johnson, 1997; Verderber and Verderber, 1992).

All too often confrontation is feared because the common use of the term implies aggression, attack, hurt, and/or destruction. While the dictionary has the common use as the first definition, it also gives the one use in communication skills, i.e., to make comparisons.

It will be helpful to the reader to consider the different types of confrontation:

- Information
- Perspectives
- Inconsistencies
- Positive
- Flaws

Information confrontation occurs when one party does not have needed information, has incomplete information, or has the wrong information. They are confronted to make them aware that they are basing their opinions or decisions on faulty input.

Perspectives confrontation will highlight disparities in the party's perceptions. It is not so much that either party is wrong, they just see things differently. The confrontation is intended to help clarify how each perceives the experience with the hope that each will appreciate and accommodate the differences.

Inconsistencies confrontation occurs when someone seems to vacillate, first expressing one perspective or opinion, and then changing to another one without seeming to be aware of the change. The confrontation is intended to show the person what he or she is saying and how it is producing confusion for the listeners. Many times individuals are not aware that they are seemingly inconsistent.

Positive confrontation invites individuals to become aware of personal resources that they seem to be overlooking and not using. The person being confronted has strengths, e.g., personality characteristics, which could be a source of positive applications. For example, a person of few words can be made aware that when he or she does contribute, the content is relevant, on target, and helpful.

Flaws confrontation is the kind that is not very helpful. It points out where the person has liabilities, shortcomings, flaws, weaknesses, etc. It is more likely to arouse defensiveness and resentment than it is to be perceived as helpful.

Group leaders will find that each of the first four types of confrontation could be used in the group. They should try very hard to not use the flaws confrontation.

Conditions for Confronting

Since confrontation is being defined as an "invitation," there are some conditions that should be in place prior to the leader using confrontation. These conditions are:

- Safety and trust
- A working or personal relationship with the person being confronted
- Current emotional state of group members at a level that would be helpful
- No personal motives for confronting

Do not confront until safety and trust are developed in the group. Trying to confront before these are established may be counterproductive as members do not feel secure enough with the leader or with each other to be willing to look critically at their behavior.

The leader should be careful to have some kind of working or personal relationship with the member being confronted. It is tempting to want to confront members who are not doing their share, arriving late, or in some way out of step with the group. These are not the members to confront, as the leader has not yet established a relationship of trust, and confrontation demands some measure of trust from both parties.

The current emotional state of all group members is also important. Any confrontation, no matter how skillfully done, can arouse intense feelings. The person being confronted may feel put on the spot, attacked, or singled-out in some way even when the leader goes out of the way to do or say nothing to suggest that. When the leader confronts, all group members will have some feelings about what is being done. They may fear that one day it will be their turn to be on the hot seat, and how the leader handles it now will determine how responsive they will be in the future. You do not want a confrontation that makes members take sides. That is counterproductive to the group and it will take considerable time and effort to overcome the negative effects.

The final condition is the leader's motive(s) for confronting. Leaders should engage in self-reflection to determine if their motives are any of the following:

- Exert power
- Manipulate
- Punish
- Seek revenge
- Show expertise
- Prove themselves "right"

If any of these are the motives, the leader should not confront. To do so would be destructive in more ways than one.

Process for Confrontation

The following are guidelines for what the confronter should do before confronting, when beginning to confront, and throughout the experience.

- Use a calm, soft voice/tone.
- Do not use words that accuse, blame, or attack.
- Assess the emotional intensity of the person being confronted. Be prepared to stop if emotions become very intense. Listening stops when emotions become intense.
- Judge whether the confrontation will benefit the person, and the group, and its task.
- Stay in touch with personal emotions and their intensity. If you feel yourself getting intense, stop.
- Give only as much information as the person can use.
- Stop if you encounter resistance or defensiveness.
- Observe the nonverbal behavior of the person being confronted and that of other group members.

- Use the guidelines for constructive feedback (next section) for what to say and how to present your thoughts.

Constructive Feedback

The most constructive feedback is that which the person can hear and use. Hearing involves lack of defensiveness, a willingness to consider what is being said, and an understanding of what is meant. Use of the information means that there is some personal investment or positive outcome for the individual. The following are suggested guidelines for making feedback constructive.

- It is descriptive or behavior without being evaluative.
- It is presented in specific terms that are observable behaviors rather than in global terms.
- The feedback is not interpretative nor does it infer motives for the behavior.
- The primary concern is for the receiver of the feedback, not the giver.
- Ideally, the feedback should be solicited rather than the giver imposing it.
- The emotional state of the receiver is important for reception, so the best feedback takes into account the timing of the feedback.
- Information in constructive feedback is limited, presented as shared information, and couched in terms that will not trigger emotional intensity.
- Feedback is concerned with what was said or done, not why.
- The presenter frequently checks with the receiver to see if what is heard is what was said, or what was meant.
- Feedback given in a group is always checked out with other members to get validation. That is, do others see the same behaviors?
- The presenter of feedback always pays attention to the consequences on the receiver.

CHAPTER 10

Group Leadership

The next set of skills discussed expand and enhance the growth and development of the group. Some are fairly easy to learn, such as giving encouragement and support, but most are more difficult, such as linking and blocking. These are more difficult because the leader first has to develop the relationship and communication skills discussed in Chapter 9 before group leadership skills can effectively be used.

This chapter bases much of the discussion on the assumption that many of the relating characteristics and communication skills presented in Chapter 9 are already developed. The group leadership skills presented here build on this foundation. Skills described include:

- Blocking
- Linking
- Questioning
- Encouragement and support
- Identification of major themes
- Directness
- Observing
- Using strengths

The chapter concludes with specific strategies for starting a session, soliciting input, mediating disputes, developing safety and trust, and ending a session.

GROUP LEADERSHIP SKILLS DEFINED

Blocking

Blocking is a skill used to protect group members, either from attacks or from proceeding in the wrong direction. It is sometimes called redirecting. Blocking is usually indicated when emotional intensity is high and/or is displaced on other members.

Sometimes when a member feels attacked or fears being attacked, he or she will displace this fear onto others to prevent being the target. The group leader has to intervene to protect both members. At other times, members ramble or tell stories instead of being focused or getting to the point. Blocking is also indicated in these situations. The leader may also need to block intensifying emotions. For example, to prevent a group member's anger from becoming fury or rage, the leader may need to intervene.

Blocking has to be done very carefully. While the intent is to keep something destructive or potentially so from escalating, the method used is also important. It is relatively easy for a leader to use sheer authority to insist that something be halted. However, the consequences of this approach are not generally positive. The member being blocked is likely to feel attacked or criticized, and other members may fear that they too will be attacked or chastised in some way. The leader is then faced with restoration of trust and safety.

To use blocking effectively, the leader should:

- Listen carefully to discern the level and intensity of emotional involvement for the individual and the group
- Gauge the strength of his or her relationship with that member and the group
- Attend to the level of emotional involvement and status for other members in the group
- Carefully select the words to use
- Approach blocking in a somewhat tentative manner

When members are in the throes of intense emotions they are very touchy or sensitive, leading to misperceptions of the leader's intent. They may become unexpectedly enraged, leaving one floundering and wondering what to do next. Awareness of the emotional status of other, less involved group members is also important, for whatever the leader does with one member is also felt by other members. It is hard to predict what will be an emotional trigger, which is why it is important to observe carefully both before and after blocking.

The strength of the relationship with the problem member and other group members is very important. The group should be at a point where it has developed some trust and safety among members and with the leader. Unless the situation is destructive or potentially very destructive, the leader should refrain from blocking too soon in the group's development.

Selection of words can be somewhat tricky. Words that have one meaning for one person can have a very different meaning for another person. Further, the leader does not want to use words that carry an implied criticism or threat. Remember, the member to be blocked is likely to be emotionally invested in the exchange and may be more sensitive than usual.

The leader should be somewhat tentative when using blocking. This will allow one to back off quickly if necessary, to select words thoughtfully, and to stay in touch with the impact on other group members. You may even want to preface blocking with a statement of intention and the reason. Doing it this way can convey to the person that the leader is not devaluing him or her, but needs to redirect the comments. For example, you could say to a storyteller, "Jane, I want to interrupt you at this point because I think your point is getting lost in details." The leader is clearly communicating the intent to block; saying it this way can provide the member with an acceptable reason for the intervention.

Linking

Group discussions can seem unnecessarily disjointed, fragmented, and chaotic at times. Of course, this perception may be correct; but on a deeper level, the group is most likely talking about something taking place in the group in an indirect way, something that the group does not feel comfortable in tackling in a direct way. In this situation the skill of linking is valuable.

Linking refers to bringing together underlying ideas, themes, concepts, and so on, whose associations are not apparent on the surface. That is, there is a commonality that is not readily discernible. The leader's job is to be detached and experienced enough to perceive these commonalities.

These commonalities of concepts, themes, etc., do not always occur in the immediate or same session; they can be exhibited over time, which is another reason why the group leader has to pay close attention. Writing a journal or even the minutes can help bring out the links.

To link, the leader must:

- Pay close attention to what happens in the group
- Remember most of what was said and by whom
- Reflect on what commonalities are being expressed, directly or indirectly
- Express the commonalities to the group, with specific examples that illustrate the associations

Questioning

Knowing when and how to question so as not to make the receiver feel attacked or defensive is a skill that can be learned. The most important aspect of this skill is learning when *not* to ask questions. That is, sometimes it is more helpful to make statements rather than ask questions. A leader needs to become aware of his or her habits and tendencies in asking questions as a major first step.

Brown (1998) points out three basic uses for questioning:

- To obtain data and information
- To clarify misunderstandings
- To pinpoint a problem in order to take immediate action (52–53)

The group leader should be especially careful to refrain from focusing on one member and pelting him or her with many questions, even if that person is talking about something where considerable clarification is needed. Many people feel attacked when they are asked many questions, regardless of the manner or tone of voice used by the asker. Thus, questioning can seem less a display of interest than a hostile interrogation. This is one of the major reasons for refraining from asking questions when possible, as one can never know whether someone will have a negative reaction. Further, much information sought by questioning is not necessary or relevant either to accomplishing the task or developing relationships in the group.

Brown (1998) lists the following as questions to be avoided:

- Limiting questions
- Hot-seat questions
- Hypothetical questions
- Disguised demands
- Masked needs
- Rhetorical questions

These kinds of questions should be avoided because they do not fulfill the basic requirement for questioning, that is, to obtain information. Limiting questions are those that require succinct answers, e.g., yes or no. Asking these may not provide all the information that is needed or available. "Hot seat" questions are designed to put the other person on the defensive. Hypothetical questions are "what if" questions, and unless you are willing to take the time to explore all the possibilities, you do not get information that you can use, or you may overlook important information. Disguised demand questions are really orders given as a question. The person really does not have much choice but to comply. Asking a question for an order can make the other person resentful. Questions that are really masked needs are very frustrating to listeners. They were asked a question but have the feeling that they are really being asked to do something for the other person, but they do not know what it is because it was not direct.

Limiting and hypothetical questions may have some small value for classroom groups. For example, limiting questions force a needed choice. If the group seems bogged down in the task and needs to make a decision, the leader can present the options in question form: "Do you want option A or option B?" Hypothetical questions can allow creative brainstorming to take place after posing a "what if" scenario. However, it is most helpful to the group if the leader explains the purpose of the hypothetical question rather than just throwing it out to the group.

In general, leaders should reserve questions for gathering facts and initiating clarifications, and limit the number of questions asked. Leaders must stay aware of the impact of questioning on the receiver and other group members, and stop when the receiver appears uncomfortable. Do not use questions to indirectly criticize or blame. It is also very important to block questioning by group members when they focus on one member and ask too many questions, to avoid making the person being questioned feel like a target.

In summary, some questions are helpful and valuable to the group's goals of learning content and developing relationships, but many are neither useful nor necessary. A good leader will learn the difference.

Encouragement and Support

Group leaders can be very helpful to the group and task accomplishment when they provide encouragement and support. This is especially crucial in the beginning stages of group, when group members are anxious and floundering because of unavoidable ambiguity.

Being too supportive, however, is counterproductive, for it promotes dependency. Also, group leaders must take care not to be supportive to meet their own personal needs. For example, if a group leader has a need to suppress, repress, or deny anger, he or she may be very supportive of group members who do not openly express anger when their nonverbal behavior is screaming that they are very upset and angry. This kind support is meeting the leader's need, but not the member's or the group's.

Giving encouragement and support will be understandably somewhat difficult for a beginning or group leader, who is likely struggling with personal insecurities about the group and competencies as leader. It may be helpful for the novice leader to think of the beginning-stage group as in a childlike stage of development. It has considerable undeveloped or underdeveloped resources, is capable of being spontaneous and creative, and is timid and tentative in a new situation. The leader is the coach that can coax members into trying new activities, the teacher that helps them see new ways of learning and knowledge, and the counselor that helps them develop their perception and awareness skills. In order to accomplish all this, members must not be left to their own devices or given orders. Every small step toward confidence should be reinforced.

To give encouragement and support, a leader can:

- Focus on positive movements and developments
- Become aware of changes and shifts members make
- Show faith in their abilities and competencies via words and deeds
- Block negative statements or attacks
- Solicit, consider, and use input from all members
- Welcome offbeat ideas
- Take pleasure in the group's progress

Identification of Major Themes

Identifying major themes for a session, a member, and the group as a whole provides the basis for linking. Themes are the unexpressed subjects or underlying basis for what is said and done. For example, a theme for a group as well as a session could be suppressing conflict. Identification would come from members' behaviors such as changing the topic whenever someone seemed to disagree, or not being truthful about feelings when asked directly.

Themes for individuals usually occur over time; the leader has to listen and remember in order to identify and report the theme. An example of a theme for an individual would be a reluctance to be direct in expressing needs, wants, or desires, such as if he or she seemed to agree with whatever other members wanted each session, but also voiced discomfort with "Yes, but . . ." statements. Both the agreement and the disagreement, of course, could be genuine. The leader would have to judge which was most important for that particular individual.

To identify themes, a leader must:

- Listen carefully and remember major topics for individuals, sessions, and the group as a whole
- Link the topics together and perceive the underlying concern or problem that they represent
- Reflect on what was said and done from a variety of perspectives
- Be tentative in reporting the theme to the group

Directness

If the leader will model speaking and responding directly to group members, then members will most likely follow that example. Part of being direct is attending to the person with whom one is talking, including orienting one's body to the other person and maintaining eye contact. Another part of being direct is to first respond in some way to what the other person has just said, via paraphrasing, reflecting, stating agreement or disagreement, or acknowledging the other's perspective. This is valuable even when one's next statement reflects a different viewpoint.

It makes people feel respected and valued when one is direct in communicating with them. Refusing to maintain eye contact, shifting around in the chair or being jumpy, fiddling with possessions, changing the topic or going off on a tangent, and presenting one's own view without first acknowledging what the other person has said are all ways that communication is not direct.

Other ways to be direct, are to:

- Openly express important feelings as they are experienced
- Give constructive feedback
- Not suppress important feelings for fear of alienating someone
- Be patient when others are talking and not interrupt

To develop directness, begin with nonverbal attending behaviors; that is, be oriented toward the other person, be present centered, maintain eye contact. Try not to be distracted, and be willing to express important feelings, when appropriate. For example, it will probably not be wise to express anger openly and directly in the beginning stages of group.

A leader can practice paraphrasing and reflecting so that they become an integral part of his or her communication style. These skills may seem somewhat artificial and redundant at first, but their use will reduce misunderstandings and miscommunications and, most importantly, make the receiver feel valued and respected.

Observing

One of the most crucial skills for the group leader to develop is observation. A member's nonverbal behaviors often convey the most truthful, accurate, and important part of the message. Content is important too, but often not as important as the nonverbal piece.

Observing the group in its entirety will take practice but will pay large dividends. The real work in the group is reflected in the group's level of participation, patterns of communication, resistance, and feeling tone. No matter what members say, the most important messages are exhibited in what the group is doing.

Participation

Level of participation refers to how active or passive members are, whether their levels of participation change, and whether participation seems forced or freely given. There are always variations in the session-to-session level of participation, and the group leader needs to be alert to changes in members' usual ways and degrees of participating. Observe how and where members sit, how much or how little they talk, and when someone suddenly decreases or increases participation.

Patterns of Communication

Patterns of communication are how the group members choose to interact with each other both verbally and nonverbally. To perceive the verbal patterns of communication, the leader should observe who talks to whom, who is ignored or interrupted, whether the leader is the nexus or conduit for messages, whether members talk directly to each other or speak generally to the group, and whether members take responsibility for what they say or not.

The nonverbal patterns of communication can be observed by watching eye contact, body orientation, and facial expressions. For example, if one member tends not to sustain eye contact with other members, then you know he or she is uncomfortable for some reason and that misunderstandings can occur because of this nonverbal behavior. The leader can help by asking the member to try to maintain eye contact when talking.

Resistance
Some forms of resistance are easy to discern while others are so subtle or hidden that it takes an expert to know that a person is resisting. What the group leader needs to know and watch for is that the group as a whole will also display resistance. Groups can resist allowing conflict to emerge, expressing intense feeling, acknowledging fears and resistances, and admitting incompetence, lack of abilities, or failure.

Some evidence of resistance surfaces when the group avoids talking about a very obvious conflict between members, makes quick changes in the topic when sensitive or emotionally charged topics emerge, has verbal clashes that do not get resolved, engages in intellectual discussions about feelings, holds there-and-then discussions instead of here-and-now ones, has long periods of uncomfortable silence, jokes or laughs inappropriately, has disputes or disagreements between members when the real conflict is with the leader, or ignores expressions of intense or uncomfortable feelings from a member.

The beginning group leader may not be able to identify resistance as such, nor will it be constructive to try to force the group to agree that it is resisting. One important point to remember is that resistance defends the group from feared destruction or abandonment. Members are not consciously aware of what they are doing. Further, each member has a unique personal basis for resistance that is also not on a conscious level. The leader will only harden the resistance, produce other defenses, or harm his or her relationship with the group by trying to attack the resistance.

The best rule of thumb for dealing with group resistance, at least in the beginning stage of a group, is to note what is happening and leave it alone. After the group has developed satisfactory relationships among members and with the leader, it can be constructive to report the resistance to the group and discuss what the group could be defending against. In sum, to point out resistance, a leader must:

• Have a satisfactory relationship with members developed over time
• Observe specific behaviors

- Report to the group only observable behaviors
- Ask group members to verify the observation
- Not judge or evaluate the behavior or members
- Not interpret or infer motives
- Be willing to drop the discussion in the face of denial or further group resistance

Feeling Tone

Feelings are important but sometimes it can be difficult to put them into words. This can be especially true for a group, as the group as a whole, not just the individual members, has a feeling tone. Why observe the feeling tone? One reason is that it tells the leader what may be important in the group but is repressed or suppressed. For example, members may be very fearful but do not openly express it or are not consciously aware that they are afraid. The fear may be of being rejected or thought to be stupid or incompetent. Until their fears are addressed, the group will remain stuck. The group leader can help by providing reassurance, encouragement, and support, but only if members voice their fears.

The leader who does not understand what the group is secretly struggling with because he or she lacks knowledge and experience will also struggle. The group will feel stuck and both the group and leader will become more frustrated. Members are caught on maintenance factors, while the leader keeps emphasizing task factors. Both think they are addressing the same thing, but they are not.

If the group leader were to tune in to the feeling tone of the group, much could be done to allay members' unexpressed fears. To tune in, the group leader should:

- Begin to allow his or her personal feelings to emerge into awareness and be identified
- Not be afraid to experience personal feelings
- Accept that personal feelings may be a reflection of what the group as a whole is feeling
- Observe what feelings are expressed verbally by members and which ones are displayed nonverbally
- Note discrepancies between what members' words and behaviors say they are feeling
- Try to label the overall feeling for each session and how it changes during the session

Using Strengths

It seems easier to focus on deficiencies and weaknesses than to emphasize strengths. Many people tend to berate themselves for what they perceive as flaws rather than being pleased about their positive points. However, almost everyone responds more positively when others recognize their strengths rather than their weaknesses. Further, others can see strengths that the person has overlooked or considered a flaw. It increases self-confidence and self-esteem when self and others focus on strengths.

The group leader can facilitate the growth and development of confidence and esteem by emphasizing and highlighting strengths and minimizing attention to flaws or weaknesses. Using this two-pronged approach can be very effective. This means that the leader must reduce or eliminate criticism, blame, and devaluing in both actions and attitudes as well as increasing awareness and attention to strengths.

Begin by increasing attention to positive aspects of oneself and others. A leader may focus on what he or she does well and, while not ignoring any perceived deficiencies or flaws, need not dwell on them. Extend this attitude to others. When you find yourself criticizing or disparaging someone, even privately, try to stop and consider something positive about the person. This will be especially helpful in the group.

To more fully use strengths, learn how a strength can be embedded in a perceived weakness, deficiency, or flaw. This strength in the flaw can be built on or up instead of remediated. Remediation is not nearly as effective as capitalizing on strengths.

Teasing out embedded strengths takes some thought and effort. Table 10.1 gives examples of possible strengths embedded in seeming deficiencies. The "criticism" category is taken from common complaints of people who work in task groups, such as those found in the classroom.

Table 10.1 Finding Strengths in Criticisms

Criticism	Possible Strength
Inability to meet target date	Attentive to details Reflective Likes to think it through
Sloppy work	Eager for action Wants to "get it done"
Ignores or overlooks details	Global thinker Sees the "big picture"
Disorganized	Pays attention to details Works sequentially
Dithers	Understands situation prior to acting Plans the entire job Organizes thoughts

Group members will appreciate the leader who seems to perceive them in a positive way and who tries to keep the focus on their strengths rather than berating them for perceived flaws.

APPLICATION OF LEADERSHIP SKILLS IN GROUP SESSIONS

It is impossible to anticipate all situations that can occur in a group in order to illustrate applications for group leadership skills. Indeed, no two groups are alike and the same group can differ dramatically from session to session, making it even more difficult to provide specific applications. What follows, therefore, are recommendations for use in five common situations:

- Starting a session other than the very first one
- Providing safety and promoting trust
- Soliciting input
- Mediating disputes
- Ending a session

Very important is how the particular members of the group interact with each other and the leader. As this cannot be known for this discussion, what follows is very general in nature and is intended to serve only as a guide.

Starting a Session

Guidelines for beginning the group and the very first session are in Chapter 2. What is presented here are suggestions for beginning other sessions. The leader should have an agenda for each session that notes what important topics need to be discussed and what tasks need to be completed. Planning is essential and is based on group needs and what emerged in the previous session.

Assume the leader has done his or her planning. The task now becomes one of starting the session. Some effective ways to start are to:

- Bring the members' attention to the here and now, by speaking to each member by name
- Set an atmosphere of task accomplishment, by asking each member to give a brief progress report
- Make each member feel a part of the group and process for task accomplishment, by presenting the agenda and requesting and using input
- Address unfinished business from the previous session, by asking individual members if concerns linger

Providing Safety and Promoting Trust

Safety and trust are two of the most important concerns for members at the beginning of the group; it takes time for members to feel safe enough to trust the leader and each other. Do not expect immediate trust. Also, do not expect members to openly and directly express their fears about safety and trust. They may not feel safe enough to tell the leader how they feel. However, these concerns are real, always present, and need to be addressed if the group is to become cohesive.

Members will feel safer when they perceive that they are a part of the group, they can see where they are headed and how they will get there, and they trust that they will be protected. The group leader's attitude is all-important in making members feel safe, and certain strategies can facilitate this process. Attitudes that help are faith that the group can be effective and that members are capable, confidence in their personal abilities even when feeling insecure about being a novice group leader, and positive regard for group members.

Specific strategies for fostering a sense of safety and trust in members are for leaders to:

- Have an agenda for each session and communicate the agenda to members
- Solicit input from all members
- Refrain from criticizing or disparaging members' ideas, even when you do not agree
- Block disparaging or criticizing remarks from other members
- Smile
- Admit to personal anxiety (without going into detail)
- Be ready to repeat directions
- Try to respond directly to members' questions
- Make reassuring and encouraging remarks
- Try not to let personal insecurities and the ambiguity of the session overwhelm them

Trust, for some members, is not easily given. By the time many students get to college they have had experiences with groups and for the most part do not like them. Add this to their unfamiliarity with the leader, instructor, and other group members and one can understand why they are somewhat tentative. Trust, like safety, is built over time and takes patience.

Members will begin to trust a leader who they feel is being truthful and genuine with them. While genuineness largely comes from within and is not a technique one can learn, a leader can at minimum provide thorough and accurate information. Members will begin to trust a leader who they sense they can rely on to take care of them and to be accurate in giving information to the best of his or her ability. The trusted leader is open and honest in verbal and nonverbal communication, does not have a hidden agenda, does not play favorites, and seeks to include all members.

Soliciting Input

Some members will be quick to voice their opinions and ideas. Others will be more tentative and will wait to be asked for their input. A group leader needs to learn and remember that there are a significant number of people who, by their training or nature, consider that if their opinion is desired it will be asked for directly. Otherwise, they think it is not needed or wanted.

Group leaders should expect to have both types in their groups and make it clear from the beginning that they are interested in input from every member. On the other hand, the leader also wants members to volunteer their input instead of having to constantly call on members for responses as a teacher would in a class. Leaders should try to avoid conducting the group as a teacher would conduct a class. Work toward a group norm of each member voluntarily contributing input as a goal, but allow that that state will take some time to develop.

Some members first have to feel comfortable with their roles in the group, with the leader, and with other group members before they are completely comfortable with volunteering their input. After all, they begin the group unsure whether they will be accepted or rejected. It is only through experience that members learn that they are valued and respected. How a leader establishes this acceptance is important.

Soliciting input begins with the very first session. The leader's behavior shapes expectations for how members will behave and relate. If the leader is content to have only some members give input, then it will be difficult to later overcome that group norm. This is one reason why the beginning group sessions are important in members' understanding of what is expected of them in the group.

To establish a group norm that each member's input is desired and expected, the group leader should:

- Value input from each member
- Respect diverse opinions
- Use input from as many group members as possible
- Try to use consensus instead of majority rule for making decisions
- Openly and directly state the desire for input from each member
- Ask members to volunteer
- Ask members who do not volunteer for their input
- Not always begin with the same person when calling on group members
- Not become too anxious with silence; pause and, if it continues, ask if members need clarification

Mediating Disputes

Specific strategies for conflict management are presented in Chapter 6. Disputes are also conflicts; they are often brief, but if the leader recognizes the potential for escalation, they can be mediated.

Mediation means that the leader stays neutral and intervenes to get the different sides talking to each other with the hope of a common outcome that will be agreeable to all. This may not be easy to do if members have strong feelings about their positions, especially if they are clashes of values. Deeply held values form our basis for how we perceive ourselves and how we live our lives. They are not easily compromised by most people whether or not they have a conscious awareness of just what their values are. Many disputes are rooted in values clashes, and a group leader has to stay aware of this.

Skills that are very useful in mediating disputes include:

- Paraphrasing
- Reflecting
- Reframing
- Clarifying
- Summarizing

These are all presented in Chapter 9. The group leadership skills of blocking and linking are also useful. Blocking is used if members begin to disparage, label, or devalue the other position, and linking is used to highlight commonalities between positions. In mediation, although most of the talk is done by members, the bulk of the work is done by the group leader. To mediate, the group leader should:

- Stay neutral
- Ask members to allow each side to state their position without comment or interruptions
- Monitor the intensity of affect for each member, including members not directly involved
- Ask each side to state their position and perception of the dispute.
- Attend to the speaker(s)
- Block inappropriate comments and remarks
- Paraphrase and reflect for one side before hearing the other side
- Try to identify commonalities
- Accept the importance of the dispute for the involved members
- Ask each side to state what it sees as a desirable outcome
- Ask each side if it can make any compromises or concessions
- Suggest a compromise outcome
- Allow members to comment on suggestions

- Directly ask each party in the dispute if the suggested compromise could be accepted
- Avoid implementing a compromise until all parties agree to it

Ending a Session

Bringing closure to each session is too often overlooked. It may be overlooked because of time constraints, but the primary reason appears to be that it is not considered important if there is another session scheduled. However, groups will stay more focused and goal-oriented if some attention is given to having a satisfactory ending to each session.

Leaders should make sure to leave a few minutes at the end of every session to close it. While you will want to preserve the designated time boundary (that is, end at the stated time) if the end of the session has arrived with no time left for the planned ending, a group leader should at least make a quick one- or two-sentence summary.

Ideally, to end a session, a group leader will:

- Summarize accomplishments
- List unfinished business or unresolved problems
- Review decisions made
- Remind members of agreements and assignments
- State when the next session is scheduled
- Thank members for their participation

CHAPTER 11

Group Activities and Exercises

Group activities, such as games and exercises, have many uses. These experiences can:

- Introduce participants and break the ice
- Formulate learning objectives
- Teach a skill
- Be fun and relieve tension
- Energize
- Increase personal awareness of behaviors and feelings
- Increase awareness of similarities and differences between group members, which promotes team development
- Integrate cognitive and affective understanding
- Bring closure

REASONS FOR GROUP EXERCISES

Introduce Participants

Most groups will be formed of members who do not know each other and will be somewhat uncertain about what they are expected to say and do. Even when members are asked to introduce themselves, they limit the amount of significant information they provide, thus ensuring that after the introductions are completed, they still do not know each other in a meaningful way. An exercise that helps break the ice and get members started talking to each other and feeling comfortable in the group can facilitate the process.

Ice breakers or introducers should be long enough to allow for an exchange of relevant information by each member and yet capable of completion within one session. "Carryovers" lack the same intensity as those that occur within one session. These exercises, while calling for exchange of significant information, should not ask for deep personal disclosures that would be embarrassing or inappropriate to share with strangers. The exercises in Chapter 2 are designed to elicit important and significant information and meet the above standard; an additional example appears at the end of this chapter.

Formulate Learning Objectives

Many students do not have a clear idea of what they would like to learn in a particular course; setting up an exercise to help them focus on personal goals and objectives that are consistent with course goals and objectives can be helpful. Students who have carefully formulated goals and objectives seem to gain more from their class experiences than students who do not. Exercises help begin the process for students to assume some responsibility for their learning and can lead to more satisfaction with instruction and personal performance.

Since classroom groups may be met with some resistance, using an exercise that gives students input into what they are expected to do and learn can aid in reducing some of the resistance. It should be noted by the instructor that whatever goals and objectives are developed at the beginning are only guides and, if not fully satisfactory, can be changed at any time by group members.

An example of this type of exercise appears in Chapter 2.

Teach Skills

Some skills can be taught using games and exercises. Communication, decision making, conflict resolution, and problem solving can be introduced, rehearsed, and reinforced through these exercises.

Using exercises to teach skills involves an understanding of the process for skills development and some knowledge of the components for the skill. For example, in order to teach conflict resolution skills the instructor must first understand and be able to use active listening skills, paraphrasing, and reflection. In addition to understanding, skills require practice. Practice means not just doing something, but doing it correctly, which means that someone who can give feedback is necessary.

An example of this type of exercise appears at the end of this chapter.

Energizers

Even the most involved group can become bogged down at times and meetings will seem to drag. It may be the result of the temperature, members feeling overwhelmed, suppressed feelings, and other conditions that contribute to the general malaise. This is when an energizing exercise could be helpful—something to get the group moving and involved.

These exercises should be short and designed to involve each member of the group without having to ask for their input. They do not have to be related to the task at all, but should be of a nature that promotes participation. You do not want to get the group off task, you just want to get a little pep into the session.

Increase Personal Awareness

Exercises are great activities for increasing individuals' awareness of their behaviors and feelings, especially in a group where there is an opportunity to get feedback from others. Rather than seeing through one's own perceptual veil, one can use the group as a mirror for what one is actually doing.

Why increase personal awareness? Increasing one's awareness is one way that personal growth happens. One can learn about one's use of self-defeating behaviors, inappropriate expression of feelings, ineffective ways of relating to others, and inefficient communication skills. Exercises and the group can provide the mechanism for interpersonal learning, leading to better self-understanding and personal growth.

Exercises used for this reason usually require expertise on the part of the leader; since one of the basic assumptions for this book is that the leader is a novice, none of these exercises are given as examples. If the leader wants to use these kinds of exercises and feels competent to do so, resources are available.

Increase Awareness of Others

Exercises are one method for helping to tune in to similarities and differences between people and to focus on and use their strengths. Immature people have a somewhat egocentric perception of the world; they assume that in order to not be perceived as prejudiced or biased they must minimize obvious differences. Still others may assume that if they ignore differences, they will disappear. None of these positions are helpful in guiding students to learn to work with a variety of disciplines and people.

Exercises can be a relatively nonthreatening way for students to increase their awareness of inaccurate assumptions and perceptions and to begin the process of their growth in understanding and toleration of diversity. They can begin to learn how to capitalize on the energy and creativity that can result from diverse viewpoints, values, and perceptions.

An exercise addressing this point appears at the end of the chapter.

Integrate Cognitive and Affective Understanding

It is relatively easy for an instructor to present cognitive content but it is less easy for a student to have both cognitive and affective understanding of the meaning of the material. For example, in group counseling classes I present the guidelines for being an effective group member, including attending all sessions and being on time. When the class first begins, students will claim that having a member miss a session or arrive late is of no consequence. After about six sessions, they begin to realize the impact of either their or other members' arriving late, and the impact of missing a session. They write about it in their journals and begin to talk about it with each other. In the beginning they had only cognitive understanding; after experiencing group work, they can better integrate their cognitive understanding with their affective understanding. Exercises do not help to develop understanding; this is something gained through experience over time and highlighted and explained by the instructor when the appropriate time comes.

Bring Closure

Just as exercises aid in breaking the ice and facilitating communication, so do they aid in helping group members realize the meaning and impact of closure. The benefits of summarizing and bringing something, such as a relationship, to a satisfactory ending are many. There are few if any loose ends, little or no unfinished business, and no lingering self-recriminations about what was not done or said.

Many groups end inappropriately and unsatisfactorily, with social events. This is one way in which members continue to deny or suppress feelings about termination. Other groups end with members just leaving, without ever acknowledging that the relationship had any positive points. There are far more constructive ways to end the group. Members need to realize that this experience, including the relationships, is over; even if they work or interact with the same people in the future, it will be a different experience. Bringing closure is neither easy nor unimportant.

An example of this type of exercise appears at the end of the chapter.

CONDUCTING GROUP EXERCISES

Basic Guidelines

While all the activities in this chapter are easy to conduct and presented in a step-by-step format, instructors may want to ask for guidance from a colleague knowledgeable about group work when first using them. It would also be helpful to take a workshop or some training in how to conduct group activities in the classroom. Basic guidelines for using exercises include giving consideration to:

- Planning
- Materials
- Physical environment

- Introducing the activity
- Processing

Planning

All activities should be planned in advance. Having said that, it should be noted that there may be times when an impromptu activity would be useful, such as when a group says it is bored. Planning, in this instance, would mean having prepared a "reserve" exercise in anticipation that it might be needed at some point.

Planning also means knowing the goal and objective for the activity. Do not use exercises just to fill time. Their impact and usefulness is wasted under those conditions. Know the purpose, the anticipated outcomes, and how the exercise will benefit the group in determining the course objectives. Each exercise in this chapter lists an objective, but group leaders are not limited to these; there may be additional objectives for their particular group.

Planning also involves gauging the right timing for an activity. Exercises are most useful when they can be tied to some obvious behavior in the group and presented close to when the behavior was exhibited. An exercise does not have to be presented in the same session as the targeted behavior, but the leader should not wait several sessions before staging the activity.

Timing also refers to allowing enough time in a session to fully complete the exercise, including sharing or feedback from each group member. The need for ample processing time is one reason why it can be beneficial to have groups of five to seven members rather than larger groups. Exercises take time not just to complete but also to process.

Another aspect of planning includes having needed materials available in sufficient amounts. Each exercise in this chapter describes what materials are needed for the activity. These should be gathered prior to the session. Few things can be more frustrating and disruptive than to have to run around at the last minute trying to find materials for an exercise. Group leaders are advised not only to gather materials but also to count them prior to the session to ensure that they are available in sufficient number for the size of the group.

Materials

In addition to simply having needed materials, leaders should also give thought to the kind of materials to be used and participants' preferences. A leader or instructor cannot always anticipate potentially important responses to the use of particular materials. For example, some group members may not like the resistance of a pencil and this dislike can influence their level of participation. Others may feel insecure about their drawing ability and, when faced with crayons or felt-tip markers, be reluctant to do anything for fear of appearing incompetent.

Distribution of materials is also a part of preparation. How and when materials will be distributed can play important roles in the effectiveness of the exercise. A good rule of thumb for making these decisions is to do it in the least disruptive manner.

Physical Environment
Along with having enough materials for each member is having a physical environment conducive to the particular exercise. For example, an exercise that requires writing also requires appropriate writing surfaces. If the exercise calls for moving around a room, then there must be enough space so that members do not fall or stumble over furniture.

It is helpful if participants can feel free to be expressive and do things that may seem silly to others. Thus, it is important to ensure privacy and freedom from intrusion. Some of the energizers, in particular, can produce feelings of embarrassment if they are inadvertently seen by someone outside the group. Members do not object to being silly with each other, but do object to being seen that way by outsiders.

Introducing the Activity
It is extremely important to introduce the activity in a way that allows members freedom to object and not participate, but that also is inviting and encouraging to participation. This is a balancing act.

Exercises should be introduced by announcing the activity, stating the objective(s), briefly describing the process, and telling members that you want their permission to continue. The leader should make it clear to members that if they do not want to do the exercise, he or she will not force them to do it. If members have reservations, the leader may get more out of the session by addressing these reservations than by continuing the exercise.

Introducing the exercise need not consume a great deal of time, but it is important to make sure members understand what will be expected. If this is a new experience for members, the leader should expect some reluctance and be ready and willing to address it.

Processing
Processing means that the leader begins a discussion on the impact of the exercise on members. Explore their feelings and thoughts in enough detail so that each member gets an opportunity to express what emerged for him or her during the experience.

Processing is very important because it is difficult to predict the impact of an exercise for anyone at a particular time. For example, one may have mild feelings surface about an exercise when not experiencing stress, but when one is under some stress, or sick, or having a crisis in an important relationship, one could have very intense feelings emerge. Or vice versa—someone under stress might keep such tight control that the feelings experienced are mild, but when he or she is relaxed, stronger feelings can emerge. Sometimes we are surprised at our own reactions, and it is no wonder that we cannot predict what will emerge for group members.

It is important to allow an opportunity for members to express intense feelings rather than trying to suppress them or leave the session without discussing them. Talking about the feelings allows members to assume more control and to feel better about themselves and the experience. Make sure that there is ample time left in the session for members to feel satisfied that they expressed their important feelings, thoughts, and ideas.

The next section presents exercises that address six categories:

- Icebreaker or introduction
- Energizing
- Tension relieving
- Teaching a skill
- Closing

Each is presented in a format that gives an objective, lists needed materials, provides a suggested introduction, describes the procedure and steps, and lists suggested processing questions and statements.

SAMPLE GROUP EXERCISES

Icebreaker or Introduction

- Exercise Name: Group Composite Seal
- Objectives: To help members begin to know each other, to build cohesiveness
- Materials: Large newsprint (11″ × 18″), crayons or felt-tips, masking tape, drawing surface (desks, tables, or walls)
- Preparation: Gather materials. Needed are 1 piece of newsprint per person and 1–2 additional sheets for the composite seal.
- Time Needed: 30 minutes
- Introduction and Procedure: Present the exercise as designed to help members know and understand each other. However, this exercise is a start at understanding how the group will be described. Following is the procedure:

   1. Each member will be given a piece of newsprint and a set of crayons or felt-tips by the group leader. Members are to draw various symbols to represent something about them, such as their greatest achievement to date. Specific categories for symbols are in section 3 of the procedure. After the individual drawings are complete, members will review their drawings and each select one symbol, cut it out, and place it on the sheet for a composite seal to represent the whole group.
   2. Stop at this point and ask if there are any questions.

3. Distribute materials; instruct members to quickly select and draw symbols or images that describe each of the following:

Their greatest achievement

A talent they have

Favorite hobby or pastime

Something that gives them pleasure

A characteristic they bring to the group that is important to them

A personal strength

A favorite possession

A value they hold

Present each item separately, pausing 20 to 30 seconds after each to allow members to draw. Have them complete all their individual drawings before selecting one symbol to add to the group composite.

Processing
After the composite drawing is complete, have members describe the symbol they chose, why they selected that one, and what it says about them and how they will relate to the group. Ask the group to give the composite picture a title.

Note to the leader: Keep the composite drawing to use in later sessions if you can, such as to help members understand how the group has changed and developed.

Energizing

- Exercise Name: Stretching
- Objectives: Focus on body and movement, bring attention to the here and now, increase personal and group energy
- Materials: None
- Preparation: Learn the directions for stretching below and ensure enough space for participants to spread their arms without hitting each other.
- Time Needed: 1 to 2 minutes
- Introduction and Procedure: Present the exercise as a way for the group to shift gears or take a break. Ask participants to stand up and go to a place in the room where they can stretch both arms out without hitting each other.

    After participants are standing in their spaces, have them slowly bring their hands together in front at about their waist, extend their clasped hands straight out, bring them up over their heads, and then separate them as far as they can without hurting. At the same time, they should raise their heads so that they look at the ceiling. The leader can demonstrate the movement before beginning. Have them hold the "stretched" position for three to five seconds and then bring their arms down to their sides. Repeat the movement and have members smile when they separate their arms. The leader can observe how individual members proceed, or can be a full participant.

Processing
Ask if members feel any different than they did before the exercise: Are they more fully present? How did it feel to stretch and smile?

- Category: Team Building
- Exercise: Count the Corners
- Objectives: Relieve tensions, demonstrate effects of competition and cooperation
- Materials: Pencils or pens and pads, envelopes, optional: prizes, stop-watch or watch with a second hand.
- Preparation:

  1. Count all corners in the meeting room including windows, light fixtures, etc., but not those for furniture and other objects.
  2. Prepare separate directions for each group member and put them in a sealed envelope. The directions are as follows. You may choose to give each member of a team (the group will be divided in teams of 2 or 3 members) the same directions or give each team member different directions. Both ways will work.

     a You are to take charge and direct the counting. You will report the results.
     b. You should count independent from the other member(s). They work separately from you.
     c. You should work cooperatively with the other members. Suggest that they divide up the room and each count in that area. You will report the results.
     d. Your team is in competition with the other team(s) and you must try very hard to beat them.
     e. Be as helpful as you can to your team. Agree with what is proposed even if you think there is a better procedure you could use. You will report the results.

- Time needed: 10–15 minutes with processing; 5 minutes if just used as an energizer with little processing.

- Introduction and Procedure: Introduce the exercise. Present it as a way to get the group moving, more in the present, and have fun when you use it as an energizer. When used to show the contrast between cooperation and competition, present it as a chance to win prizes if you use them, or as a way to learn to work in a team.
- Describe the rest of the procedure as presented below.

    a. The group will be divided in teams of 2–3 members.
    b. Each member will be given a sealed envelope with directions and instructed to read the directions but not to reveal them.
    c. The task for each team is to count all the corners in this room, excluding furniture and other objects.
    d. Time given for completion is _____. (The leader can choose how much time to give. Recommended is 2–3 minutes).
    e. The winner will be judged on both time needed to complete the task and accuracy.

The leader should pause at this point and answer any questions.

Proceed to divide group in teams and distribute envelopes. Have members wait until all envelopes are distributed before opening them. Note the time and give the signal to begin. Call time and have each team report their findings. Select a winner if you choose to, or just begin to process the experience.

- Observations: The leader can observe how the teams carry out the exercise to report back to the group during processing. For example, did the team discuss how to proceed before beginning to count or did each member just begin to count? Did the room get divided up or did the entire team count the same area? How did members appear, e.g., frustrated, energized, etc.?

Processing
- When used as an energizer, confine the processing to having members respond to what the experience was like for them and are they feeling more energized now. It will also be helpful to have all members read their directions if different ones are used for each.

When used to show the effects of cooperation and competition begin with the same response as when used as an energizer. Extend the discussion to include how members feel about having different directions and what they experienced as they tried to complete the task. The most likely team to be the winner or closest is the one with the directions given in C, but you cannot be positive this will happen. If C is the winner then you will find it easy to point out the impact of team members being cooperative. If others are the winners, you can then explore with the group their thoughts on being more effective if the teams had instructions to be cooperative.

- Variations: Give all members of a team the same instructions. Give all teams the same instructions. Use only 2–3 of the 5 instructions.

Tension-Relieving

- Exercise Name: Faces and Feelings
- Objectives: Help participants become more aware of feelings displayed by facial expressions, show how congruence of feelings and gestures is manifested, have fun, relieve tension
- Materials: None
- Preparation: Read directions below and be familiar with them
- Time needed: 5 to 15 minutes
- Introduction and Procedure: Introduce the exercise by telling participants the objectives. The procedure will be that one member begins the process by forming a facial expression to exhibit his or her current emotional state. The next person must first assume the same expression and then change expression to reflect his or her own current emotional state. The person who is assuming an expression should then turn so that the next person can see his or her face. Ask participants to note what expressions are displayed.
- Processing: Ask each member to describe how easy or hard it was to take on someone else's expression and how it felt to assume an expression reflective of current emotion. Other items to explore are whether their feelings changed from the time the exercise was introduced to the moment it was their turn, and what feelings they saw reflected on members' faces. Make sure that the last is verified by the person being reflected. It can be useful to see how accurate the guesses are. It can also be instructive to see how feelings changed as the exercise progressed, if members edited or changed their expressions and were not open about their real feelings, or if someone was unable to identify his or her own emotion.

Teaching a Skill—Problem Solving

- Exercise Name: Getting What You Need
- Objectives: To teach members how to determine needed resources and how to negotiate for them, to understand the positive aspects of cooperation versus competition
- Materials: For each group, two pairs of scissors, two rulers, two glue sticks, two rolls of string, one set of felt-tip markers, 8.5″ × 11″ poster

board (one piece per group member), assorted colored sheets of paper (six white, four blue, one red, one gold, one black, two green), large manila envelopes (one per group member), tables as desks.
- Preparation: The above materials should be divided somewhat randomly and placed into envelopes, one for each group member. Each group member should have a different set of materials. Five possible sets are presented below as examples (assuming a group size of five).

1. Five (or number of group members) pieces of poster board, two sheets colored paper (red and blue)
2. Scissors, glue stick, string, felt-tip markers
3. Ruler, string, three sheets of paper (gold, white, and black)
4. Five sheets of white paper, three sheets of blue paper
5. Scissors, ruler, two sheets of green paper, glue stick

Separate each set of materials and place in a large envelope with the following directions. Each group member's envelope should have a different set of materials, but all members will receive the same instructions (in the instructions, N means number of group members).

Each member will receive a different set of materials. You will have 20 minutes to produce the following:

N white paper containers

N paper shapes made up of smaller versions of the same shapes, e.g., a triangle made of triangles

N 3" diameter circles

N paper collages or pictures using no less than four colors

N 12" garlands made of blue paper links

- Time needed: one hour
- Introduction and Procedure: Present the exercise as an activity designed to demonstrate problem-solving strategies. Tell members that each will be given a different set of materials and each is expected to make the objects on the list. Tell them that there are enough materials in each group to make all of the objects and it is their task to find out (problem solve) how to accomplish it. The first person to complete all objects wins.

Stop at this point and answer questions. Distribute materials and give the signal to begin.

The leader should observe how the group chooses to go about the task. Do they jump in and begin constructing immediately? Does someone make a suggestion about procedure that is accepted and acted on? Do members seem reluctant to begin or make suggestions? As they begin construction of the objects, do they talk with each other? Does anyone volunteer to share? Do they put all materials in the center so that everyone can have access? Does each member make the objects or do they divide the task so that 1 or 2 make all of one object, such as the garland?

- Processing: Focus the discussion on how members felt about the task when they saw the directions and their materials, while engaged in construction, and when the final products emerged.

    The leader then reports observations and invites discussion on the effectiveness and efficiency of the group's problem-solving strategy.

Closing

- Exercise Name: Say Goodbye
- Objectives: Increase awareness of accomplishments, complete unfinished business, end the group
- Materials: A variety of pictures from catalogs and magazines, one sandwich bag for each member, glue sticks, felt markers, one 5 × 8 card for each group member, scissors
- Preparation: Cut pictures from catalogs and magazines of objects, animals, colors, and other images. Select several different pictures and place in sandwich bags. Secure other materials.
- Time needed: One hour
- Introduction and Procedure: Present the exercise as a way to reflect on what the group has accomplished and how members have experienced each other. Distribute the materials and ask that each member make a collage using cutout images to represent symbolically each of the following:

1. The group's accomplishment of its goal
2. The member's own participation
3. Each other member, as the artist perceived or experienced them

    Tell members they can use the felt markers to draw a symbol if they do not have a fitting one in their bags. They are also free to share pictures. Tell them they have ten to fifteen minutes to complete their collage. (Most of the time is needed for processing, not construction.)
- Processing: Ask members to show their collages and explain the symbols. Do not probe for meaning but ask clarifying questions if necessary. Most of the time should be given for members' explanations. After all are finished, ask each, "How do you want to say good-bye to the group?"

CHAPTER 12

Electronically Linked Groups

Groups can be linked electronically by video, telephone, and computer, via the Internet. Electronically linked groups do not have to meet some of the criteria that groups who meet face-to-face do, such as scheduling times for meetings when all members can attend; holding meetings at an approved site; and requiring members to attend sessions, arrive on time, and not leave early. Electronically linked groups also have different structural and directing needs than do on-campus classroom groups. If such groups' unique characteristics and needs are considered when planning, they can be very effective and provide a rich learning experience.

SPECIFIC CHARACTERISTICS OF ELECTRONICALLY LINKED GROUPS

Regardless of the means of electronic linkage, these groups have several common characteristics, advantages, and disadvantages. Many, or even most, electronically linked classroom groups will meet via the computer. Some groups may have access to video conferencing hardware, but even these groups may need to use the computer for some meetings. Since a computer link is likely to be the most common format, much of the following discussion is based on that assumption, though most of the information provided here also applies to other kinds of electronically linked groups.

The basic characteristics of electronically linked groups are that:

- Meetings can be held at any time
- Members can be located anywhere in the world
- Members are free to exit sessions at any time
- Interactions are not face to face

- The quality and availability of equipment are essential
- Most members will be physically isolated
- Few, if any, opportunities for informal or impromptu interactions will arise
- The need for clarification, guidance, and instructions must be anticipated by the leader and instructor
- It is more difficult to perceive both the "whole" and how each individual contributes (Brown & Cross, 1999)

Meeting Times and Places

Meetings of electronically linked groups can literally be held at any time. The entire 24 hours in a day are now available and members can arrange meetings around the other activities, needs, and demands in their lives. This convenience can be extremely important for students who must work, have child care responsibilities, or other classes.

Another convenience is that students do not have to travel to have group meetings. This also relieves pressure from the other responsibilities they may have. Further, the necessity for finding appropriate meeting places is eliminated, which is one less constraint.

Location of Members

Members of electronically linked groups can be widely dispersed throughout the world, including the middle of the ocean. On the other hand, more organization is needed to set meeting dates and times, especially when members are located in various time zones. Planning, therefore, becomes even more important.

Freedom to Exit

When meeting via computer (although not via telephone or video), there is no way to know if a member is present, absent, or simply choosing not to participate actively. Thus members are freer to exit a session. They do not have to say anything or see others' reactions; they simply leave and no one is the wiser. Students' honesty and sense of responsibility, therefore, play major roles in electronically linked groups.

Interactions

Electronic interactions are not face to face, nor do they provide many of the other visual and auditory clues we rely on for communicating. Metacommunication, or the subtext of meaning in communications, is severely impacted. There are numerous other implications and influences of electronic meetings on communications that have serious consequences for group interactions.

These are discussed in more detail in the sections below on advantages and disadvantages.

Equipment

Electronically linked groups are not possible without adequate equipment, usually computers. This means that the hardware must be up to date and in good working condition, or nothing will happen. However, there are other technical difficulties that can occur that will impact such group work, including, for example, bad weather.

Physical Isolation

It is difficult to consider oneself a member of a group when one is physically isolated. Despite expectations to interact, contribute, work on a task, and so on with others, the reality is that one sees and hears no one else; one is alone. The effect on group members, group dynamics, and the task have not been researched, but it is logical to expect that physically isolated members of electronically linked groups will perceive the group and its task differently than do members of groups that meet and interact face-to-face.

Informal Interactions

Members of teams and groups feel more connected to them when they know other individual members. Much of the first few group sessions generally focuses on helping members become acquainted. Groups that meet face-to-face have an advantage for accomplishing this task that electronically linked groups do not: informal and impromptu interactions that occur spontaneously when individuals are in the same vicinity.

Informal interactions can allow members to know each other's hobbies, pastimes, likes and dislikes, attitudes, beliefs, and opinions on a variety of topics. In short, they learn about each other from topics unrelated to the task. Becoming acquainted reduces uncertainty and promotes trust. When members do not have an opportunity to get to know group members from something other than the task, they remain more aloof, more detached, possibly less committed.

Anticipated Needs for Guidance

Not everything a group will need can be anticipated. However, electronically linked groups are already dealing with considerable ambiguity, frustration, and anxiety because of physical remoteness and isolation. If careful planning has not been done to anticipate group needs, all those feelings intensify and escalate. Members are then dealing with the unknown with little or no reassurance or support. The task will seem overwhelming to them.

Instructors who devote time and effort to plan and anticipate what groups need to know, what materials are needed, how to delineate processes and procedures, what barriers and constraints may exist and how to overcome or compensate for these, and other guidance will reap considerable benefits in the long run. Their class groups will function better, students will learn more, and the students and instructor will feel greater satisfaction for what was done and accomplished.

Global versus Specific

Students generally have difficulty at first in understanding the "whole" picture and this difficulty is compounded for electronically linked groups. Their isolation and remoteness contribute to this difficulty, for they have no one readily available with whom to explore their confusion.

Group work demands that there be a group project, accomplishment, or outcome as a goal. Each individual member contributes to attaining the goal, but all must first understand what the final product will be and how each piece fits in. Since many, or most, students will be unfamiliar with working in groups, or have had unproductive experiences in groups, the instructor has to understand that many of the gripes, expressions of confusion, and frustrations are not a result of the task itself but of the students' need to see the "whole."

COMMON CHARACTERISTICS OF ELECTRONICALLY LINKED AND CLASSROOM-BASED GROUPS

Electronically linked groups have much in common with other types of groups. Instructors need to be aware of these commonalities and anticipate how to manage and control them so that the focus of class is not lost, but enhanced by the use of groups. Basic shared characteristics are:

- Developmental stages
- Members seeking to connect and communicate
- Decisions made even when the group decides not to decide
- Conflict and controversy
- Development of a set of overt and covert group norms

Electronically linked groups will move through the same stages as do other groups: beginning, conflict, cohesion, and termination; it may be more difficult, however, to determine where one stage ends and another begins. It is relatively easy to perceive the first and last stages, but not as easy for the middle stages. What is important is that the instructor anticipates and plans for certain behaviors associated with group stage in order to prevent or eliminate problems. See Chapter 5 to review group stages.

ADVANTAGES AND DISADVANTAGES OF ELECTRONICALLY LINKED GROUPS

Johnson and Johnson (1997) list the following as feelings and attitudes common to members of electronically linked groups:

- Members can become detached from their peer audience
- Members may be less constrained by the usual social and cultural norms for communication and behavior
- Members feel a greater sense of anonymity
- Members are less able to perceive each other as individuals
- Members exhibit less empathy
- Members may be less concerned about comparisons with others

There are both positive and negative consequences for members and the group as a result of these feelings and attitudes. These consequences help define the advantages and disadvantages of electronically linked groups, discussed below.

Advantages

Table 12.1 presents some primary advantages for electronically linked groups. These are categorized as structural and member advantages. Structural advantages refer to characteristics that promote ease of group meetings and communication; member advantages describe how interactions and behaviors are more positive in electronically linked groups.

Structural Advantages
As noted before, meetings can be held at any time and members' schedules can be more easily accommodated. Electronic communications need not be timebound; that is, members can communicate at their convenience. What we generally think of as group meetings become more the sending and receiving of messages, not necessarily during a synchronous time frame. Members can also be in groups no matter where they are geographically. Meeting times can be shorter, which can contribute to greater efficiency and effectiveness.

Member Advantages
The format of electronically linked groups can be very beneficial in promoting member participation. Whereas some members may be shy or fearful of talking in a group, they become less so when they are able to be alone. They feel freer to express their thoughts, opinions, and ideas because they are free from distractions, such as facial expressions that may appear to be discouraging.

How members interact is also positively affected. For example, members will be less influenced by prestige and status, leading to more willingness to give their input which, in turn, promotes greater and more equal participation.

Table 12.1 Advantages of Electronically Linked Groups

Structural
Meetings can be held at any time.
Communication can be faster.
Communication and meetings can be asynchronous.

Member
Members feel freer to express thoughts and feelings.
Participation can be more equalized.
Participation is less affected by prestige and status.
A group norm of only one member speaking at a time is less likely.
Relationships are not confounded by personal appearances.
The tendency to stereotype others is reduced.
Geographical and chronological flexibility gives members freedom and improves attitudes toward group work.
Members may be more willing to share unconventional ideas that promote creativity.
Members may be more comfortable in dress.

Members are also less likely to develop a group norm of having only one member speak at a time since the format does not discourage or allow interruptions. Members can respond whenever they want.

Another benefit is that lack of visual connections can allow members to react to each other without stereotyping because of race or ethnic group, personal appearance, or other status cues. By the time any of this may be known, it is less likely to influence personal perceptions.

The opportunity to participate from anywhere in the world and at any time can have a profound effect on members' attitudes about group work. Personal schedules and family responsibilities can be more easily accommodated, thereby reducing concern and anxiety that can negatively impact performance.

All groups can benefit from open expression of unconventional ideas and creative input. However, it can be daunting for students to propose something that is a little offbeat to their group of peers when they are meeting face to face. It is easier to read or misread nonverbal behavior and interpret it as disapproval or rejecting. When nonverbal cues are absent it is less threatening for members to propose different ideas since all the cues for what members are thinking are written. This alone can make the process less threatening. Electronically linked groups have the potential for opening up the discussion to consideration of unconventional ideas that can provide some creative solutions or directions.

Comfort in dress is very important for some students, and for most electronically linked groups, members can attend meetings dressed as they wish.

Disadvantages

Although there are many advantages and benefits to electronically linked groups, there are some disadvantages that should be considered. Many of them occur because of the lack of visual and auditory contact, the loss of the immediacy of synchronous communication, and the physical isolation of electronic meetings. Table 12.2 lists some of the disadvantages.

The disadvantages are categorized as individual member and group-level conditions, though there is overlap between the two. Individual member disadvantages are behaviors and attitudes that are exhibited or most acutely felt by individual members of an electronically linked group. Group-level conditions more likely affect the group-as-a-whole because of the unique characteristics of electronically linked groups.

Table 12.2 Disadvantages of Electronically Linked Groups

Individual Member

Members may not observe social conventions leading to potentials for sexual and racial harassment.

Feelings of detachment and isolation for members.

Members can feel that they are not perceived or accepted as individuals.

Less, or lack of, empathy.

Group-Level

There is a tendency to lose focus.

Leader is remote, leading to lack of power and control and slowing development of safety and trust.

Metacommunication and immediacy are missing providing more opportunities for misunderstandings, miscommunications and misinterpretations.

More difficult to establish and maintain appearances of objectivity and fairness for instructor.

Instructors have less opportunity to observe and intervene.

Individual Member Disadvantages

The most troubling condition that can occur is that members may not observe usual and acceptable social conventions. They do not know each other and, because they cannot see the impact of what they are doing or saying on others, can be or at least seem indifferent to the others' feelings and needs. Members will feel freer to communicate thoughts and feelings, and communicate them in ways that they ordinarily would not. This can lead to harassment intended or perceived. For example, some members may use profanity, make sexually explicit comments, or use racially derogatory words and phrases that they would not use when talking directly to another person. Thus, it is important that there be specific guidelines for how students are expected to communicate as members of an electronically linked group and for the penalties for violations.

Members can easily feel detached and isolated since they neither see nor hear other group members. It is much more difficult to get a feeling of "groupness" than it is when members meet face-to-face. There may be less connection and commitment to the group because of the inability to sense that there is a group. An instructor will have to work very hard to have each group member realize and accept that he or she is perceived as an individual. This is important even when groups meet face-to-face, as the tendency is to feel that individuals are overlooked and only the group is important, which intensifies the feelings of detachment and isolation.

It is also easy to be less empathic with fellow group members, as the cues to the emotional content for messages are missing. We tend to gauge the emotional intensity of a message from nonverbal gestures, tone of voice, and some sort of connection with the person. All of this is reduced or missing for electronically linked groups.

Group-Level Disadvantages

Group-level disadvantages affect the entire group and not just a few members. These conditions may not have any solution, but some can be anticipated and their impact reduced or eliminated.

Electronically linked groups tend to lose focus more easily, as it takes longer for them to perceive the task and their roles or contributions. The usual give-and-take that sorts out the essentials may not be present unless the instructor plans for it. Once a group gets on the wrong track or loses its focus, it is very difficult to recover. Recovery takes time from accomplishment of the task.

The leader of an electronically linked group may become frustrated because, in part, he or she is remote from members and from the instructor. This remoteness contributes to a sense of lack of power and control, making it easy for a leader to feel that there is chaos instead of order. Further, electronic distance makes it harder to develop trust and safety among all the members of the group, including the leader, yet until the group begins to trust the leader and to feel safe, it does not become cohesive or productive.

The lack of metacommunication leads to serious group problems. When members cannot see or hear each other, much subtext is lost. It is easy to underestimate the amount of information we take in and use through our eyes and ears, so that when one or both of these channels of communication are absent, we tend to flounder, feel confused, and ascribe or project our personal meanings instead of trying to clarify what the other person meant.

For example, when communications are face-to-face we tend to observe and give importance to nonverbal gestures to cue us as to the "real" meaning. We listen to the tone of voice; notice the body, arm, and leg positions; note any nervous movements; judge sincerity by the degree of eye contact; and place considerable importance on facial expression. All of this is missing in communication between members of an electronically linked group.

Thus, the lack of metacommunication clearly leads to more opportunities for misunderstandings, miscommunications, and misinterpretations to occur. The leader cannot overestimate impact of these on:

- Developing safety and trust
- Constructive resolution of conflicts
- Feeling a part of a group
- Accepting and respecting group members
- Having a commitment to the group and its task

When the immediacy of synchronous interaction is absent, opportunities to clarify are reduced or eliminated, leading to more misunderstandings. Immediacy promotes clarification. The speaker can see that the other person is confused, or the listener makes a comment that lets the speaker know at once that there is some misunderstanding. Since these cues are missing in an electronic meeting, the advantage of immediacy to accurate understanding is lost.

Instructors also suffer some disadvantages with important implications. First, it is more difficult to establish and maintain appearances of objectivity and fairness. The instructor may indeed be fair and objective, but that also has to be the perception of the students, and the physical separation can have a very negative impact on their perception of objectivity and fairness. In addition, students cannot see the instructor, get to know him or her, and, in many cases, hear about him or her through the campus grapevine. All these factors may contribute to skepticism about the instructor's ability to be fair and objective.

Instructors will feel the lack of opportunity to observe groups in action or intervene with immediacy. A considerable amount of information is available to instructors about individual participation, group functioning, and task accomplishment through observation, which allows him or her to intervene expeditiously to steer groups in the right direction, prevent conflicts from escalating, and generally keep things moving smoothly. However, for most electronically linked groups, the instructor can intervene only after the situation becomes so acute that the instructor's help is sought or conditions are so bad that they cannot be ignored.

INSTRUCTOR TASKS AND STRATEGIES

Many instructor tasks and strategies will be similar to those for on-campus groups. However, there are some that are unique for electronically linked groups and others that must be modified for these groups. For example, planning is common to both types of groups but may need some adaptation for electronically linked groups, such as providing more extensive guidelines. The guidelines provided in earlier chapters also hold for electronically linked groups and their members.

The major tasks and strategies are to:

- Provide sufficient structure
- Have visual connectors for the class and groups
- Develop personal linkages
- Develop a fair and equitable evaluation and reward plan
- Monitor electronic meetings

Sufficient Structure

Just as with other groups, members of electronically linked groups should receive a detailed syllabus, written guidelines for participation and the project, and rules of conduct. The instructor should take care to anticipate what information will be needed and give enough detail so that questions will be reduced. It is even more important that the syllabus and guidelines be reviewed with students who are at a distance, since there are fewer opportunities to have informal clarification chats. Fax, phone, and e-mail are helpful, but cannot fully take the place of face-to-face communication.

It is also important for the instructor to have regular office hours for the distant student, when he or she will be available to communicate and interact via phone or e-mail. Students need to be able to count on the availability of the instructor at specified and regular times.

The instructor must also arrange for meetings with group leaders and, if possible, hold group meetings. These can be via electronic means, just as the student groups meet. It is advisable for these meetings to be held at least twice a month on a regular schedule.

Visual Connectors

This is a strategy that can facilitate feelings of commitment and cohesion to the group for members. Visual connectors can be group symbols or names, a group logo, a class image, and copies of class or group members' work.

Group symbols or group names would be identifiers similar to those used by sport teams, schools, or colleges. For example, a group symbol could be an animal that is symbolic of how the members identify the group (tigers), and a group name might be similar (the Fighting Tigers).

A group logo follows the same illustrative principles, but the logo is a more abstract symbol that tries to incorporate the essence of what the group is about. It could even be a coat of arms that displays several symbols associated with the group.

The instructor could develop a class image that appears on all documents, or have each group develop an image of the group that would appear on all their work. These would be easy identifiers that could promote feelings of cohesion and belonging.

The last suggestion for a visual connector is expensive to implement but can reduce feelings of isolation and promote a sense of fairness. If possible, the instructor can reproduce copies of individuals' work and distribute it to other class members, or just to other group members. Thus, each member of a class or of a group gets to see what others' products are like, which gives everyone some basis for comparisons.

Personal Linkages

Providing opportunities for personal linkages for group members is a very important strategy for instructors of electronically linked groups. Doing one or more of the following will help group members get to know each other on a more personal basis and reduce feelings of not being perceived as an individual.

- Develop a form for exchange of personal information (hobbies, favorite TV shows, etc.).
- Have each group member send a picture to the instructor, who then compiles them into a group picture and distributes it to each member.
- Use short exercises to help members become acquainted.
- Have members gather pictures from magazines that are representative of or important or significant to them. Members send all the pictures to the instructor or group leader, who then develops a group collage and distributes copies to each member.

Evaluation and Reward Plan

This is a critical part of the syllabus and should be highlighted during its review. Students are understandably anxious about how they will be evaluated, especially when their grade is dependent on how well other group members perform. In addition, the instructor should confront individuals who are not performing or whose performance is substandard; be consistent and fair in insisting that all group members are accountable and held responsible; and ensure that there is appropriate reward for individual performance as well as group performance.

Monitor Electronic Meetings

An instructor cannot explain the directions and group structure and then just let groups work on their own. It is essential that the instructor monitor these groups. Monitoring provides an extra measure of safety for group members, keeps the group on task, and lets the instructor know of potential problems before they become acute. This is important for all classroom groups, but even more so for groups that meet by electronic means.

Some monitoring strategies for the instructor are to:

- Require that the instructor be notified in advance of all meetings
- Drop in to meetings unannounced
- "Lurk," that is, attend a meeting without saying anything and just observe
- Require that minutes be submitted to the instructor for all meetings
- Provide extensive guidelines for acceptable behaviors in order to prevent harassment

FORMING ELECTRONICALLY LINKED GROUPS

The processes for forming classroom groups cannot be applied when forming electronically linked groups. Where group members are located, how they are expected to communicate, and the nature of the task or project play a part in deciding how to form such groups, but regardless of these, six major considerations apply:

- Size of the group
- Determination of membership
- Guidelines and resources
- Evaluation policies
- The first meeting
- Rules for conduct

As with classroom groups, the size of electronically linked groups should be limited to five to eight members each. There are several advantages to keeping the groups small.

- Scheduling meetings is easier.
- Members are less likely to get lost in anonymity.

- Interaction is easier.
- More task involvement and sense of responsibility exist for the group and its task.
- Fewer constraints are imposed on sharing opinions and ideas.

In distant learning, if there are sufficient members at one particular site the instructor may want to make them a group. However, there is at least one major disadvantage to doing that, as group members may already have some experiences with each other that were less than positive. Thus, there is existing conflict in the group about which the instructor knows nothing but which will have a negative impact on the functioning of the group. Still, the advantages may outweigh the disadvantages.

More likely, however, is that members will be geographically separated. In this case, the instructor should make every effort to form groups by random assignment of members. Random assignment could be done by taking the printed roll; deciding on the number of groups; giving each student a group number (e.g., 1, 2, 3); and putting all 1's in a group, and so on. This process could also integrate some campus-based students with distant students in a group.

Give extensive written guidelines to group members; an instructor cannot provide too much detail. Guidelines should be written for governing member behavior in the group, expectations for accomplishing the task, and how and when to obtain needed resources. If there are penalties for violations, these should be highlighted.

The importance of providing clear evaluation procedures cannot be overemphasized, especially for students at distant sites. Provide a scheme for judging quality of group participation as well as task accomplishment. Grade both individual effort and group outcomes.

The instructor will have to structure the first group meeting, as he or she probably will not have time to meet with group leaders and allow them to decide on the structure. Be sure to have a get acquainted exercise to help group members begin to know each other as individuals; ask students to discuss their personal goals for the class and how these can be incorporated in the group goals; and help members set meeting dates and times to be consistent with course guidelines.

Establish clear rules for how students are expected to behave as group members. Refer to university regulations or even send them a copy. Many academic institutions have policies in place to govern student to student electronic interactions and these should be made known to students. Some specific rules that should be emphasized.

- There is zero tolerance for sexual or racial harassment.
- Members are expected to attend all meetings.

- The instructor must be fully informed about all meetings.
- Some interactions may contain confidential material but the instructor is to be considered a member of the group and kept fully informed via minutes or other means.
- Each member is expected to participate and contribute to accomplishing the task.

Bibliography

Brown, N. 1996. *Expressive processes for group counseling.* Westport, CT: Praeger.

Brown, N. 1998. *Psychoeducational groups.* Philadelphia, PA: Accelerated Development.

Brown, N. & J. Cross. 1999. Electronically linked groups for engineering students. Presentation at the American Society for Engineering Education International Conference, Charlotte, NC.

Carroll, M., M. Bates, & C. Johnson. 1997. *Group leadership,* 3rd ed. Denver, CO: Love Publishing Group.

Corey, M. S. & G. Corey. 1998. *Becoming a helper,* 3rd ed. Pacific Grove, CA: Brooks-Cole.

Daniels, V. & L. J. Horowitz. 1984. *Being and Caring,* 2nd ed. Palo Alto, CA: Mayfield.

Forsyth, D. R. 1999. *Group dynamics,* 3rd ed. Belmont, CA: Wadsworth.

Freeberg, N. & D. Rock. 1987. Development of a small-group team performance taxonomy based on meta-analysis. Final report to the Office of Naval Research. In D. W. Johnson & F. P. Johnson, eds., *Joining together.* Boston: Allyn and Bacon.

Gazda, G., F. R. Ashbury, F. J. Balzer, W. C. Childers, R. E. Phelps, & R. P. Walters. 1995. *Human relations development,* 5th ed. Boston: Allyn and Bacon.

Gladding, S. T. 1995. *Group work a counseling specialty.* Englewood Cliffs, NJ: Merrill.

Hafen, B. Q., K. J. Karren, K. J. Frandsen, & N. L. Smith. 1996. *Mind/Body Health.* Boston, MA: Allyn & Bacon.

Johnson, D. B. & R. Johnson. 1992. *Positive interdependence: The heart of cooperative learning.* Edina, MN: Interaction Book.

Johnson, D. B. & R. Johnson. 1994. *Leading the cooperative school,* 2nd ed. Edina, MN: Interaction Book.

Johnson, D. W. & F. P Johnson. 1997. *Joining together,* 6th ed. Boston: Allyn and Bacon.

Katzenbach, J. & D. Smith. 1993. *The wisdom of teams*. Cambridge, MA: Harvard Business Press.

Meisgeier, C., E. Murphy, & C. Meisgeier. 1989. *A teacher's guide to type: A new perspective on individual differences in the classroom*. Palo Alto, CA: Consulting Psychologists Press.

Pheiffer, J. W., Ed. *Annual handbook* (1970–2000) San Francisco: Jossey-Bass/Pfeiffer.

Scannell, E. E. & J. N. Newsome. 1983. *More games trainers play*. New York: McGraw-Hill.

Tarvis, C. 1989. *Anger: The misunderstood emotion* NY: Touchstone.

Tuckman, B. & M. Jensen. 1977. Stages of small group development revisited. *Group and organizational studies* 2: 419–427.

Tuckman, B. 1965. Developmental sequence in small groups. *Psychological Bulletin*, 63: 384–399

Verderber, R. R. & K. S. Verderber. 1992. *Interact,* 6th ed. Belmont, CA: Wadsworth.

Webster's new universal unabridged dictionary, 2nd ed. 1983. New York: Dorset and Baber.

Worchel, S., D. Coutant-Sassic, & M. Grossman. 1992. A developmental approach to group dynamics: A model and illustrative research. In S. Worchel, W. Wood & J. Simpson, eds., *Group process and productivity*. Newbury Park, CA: Sage.

Yalom, I. 1995. *The theory and practice of group psychotherapy,* 4th ed. New York: Basic Books.

Index